Spain Uncovered:

A Traveler's Odyssey Through Iberian Splendor | Culture, History, And Enchanting Destinations Await

Finnian Asherwood

© **Copyright 2024 - All rights reserved.**

Without the publisher's or author's explicit written consent, it is illegal to copy, reproduce, or transmit any part of this work.

Damages, recovery, or financial loss resulting from the information provided in this book are not the responsibility of the publisher or author. No way, either directly or indirectly.

Legal Notice:

Copyright safeguards this book. Please do not distribute this book to anyone. Without the author's or publisher's permission, you are not allowed to copy, distribute, sell, use, quote, or paraphrase any portion of this work.

Disclaimer Notice:

Keep in mind that the content of this paper is meant solely for educational and recreational purposes. This information has been compiled with the utmost care to ensure its accuracy, timeliness, reliability, and completeness. Neither express nor implied warranties of any kind are herein made. This material is not intended to provide medical, financial, legal, or any other type of expert advice. A number of sources have contributed to the material of this book. If you are not an expert in your field, you should not try any of the methods outlined in this book.

Please note that the author cannot be held responsible for any damages, whether they are direct or indirect, that may result from the use of this text. This includes any errors, omissions, or inaccuracies that may be contained within.

Table of Contents

Introduction 5

Chapter 1: Travel Essentials 7

    Best time to visit. 7

    What to pack 9

Chapter 2: Must Visit Places in Spain 27

    These are the top ten places in Spain that you simply must see 29

        Barcelona 29

        Madrid 30

        Granada 31

        Seville 31

        Bilbao 32

        Valencia 32

        Burgos 32

        Corboda 33

        egovia 33

        Spanish Islands 34

    Famous Architectural Wonders to Visit in Spain 34

        City of Arts and Science 35

        Metropol Parasol 35

        Guggenheim Museum 36

        Torre Glories 36

Bridge Pavilion 36

Oscar Niemeyer International Cultural Centre 36

Hotel Marques de Riscal... 37

Concert Hall 37

Museo Del Prado 37

Barcelona's Sagrada Familia and Gaud Locales 38

The Incomparable Mosque of Cordoba (La Mezquita)........... 39

The Prado and Paseo del Artes, Madrid................................. 40

San Lorenzo de El Escorial 40

Seville Basilica and Alcázar... 41

Guggenheim Gallery, Bilbao.. 42

Santiago de Compostela House of God 43

Court Mayor, Madrid.. 44

Court de Espaa and Parque de Mara Luisa, Seville 45

Ciudad de las Artes y las Ciencias, Valencia 45

Gran Canaria's beaches.. 46

La Rambla, Barcelona.. 47

El Teide, Tenerife... 47

Toledo's Old City 48

Chapter 3: Itineraries 50

Why you need itinerary.. 50

one-week itinerary 52

two-week itinerary 55

Weekend Itinerary: Barcelona, Catalonia............................. 58

Chapter 4: Best Restaurants and Cuisine 61

Culinary Techniques & Traditions: 61
Regional Variations & Specialties: 61
Key Ingredients & Staples: 62
Desserts, Pastries & Sweets: 62
Restaurants 65

Chapter 5: Accommodations in Spain 72

1. Hotels & Resorts: 72
2. Hostels & Budget Accommodations: 73
3. Vacation Rentals & Apartments: 74
4. Paradores & Historic Lodgings: 75
5. Campsites & Glamping: 76

Chapter 6: Cultural Activities in Spain 78

Chapter 7: Nightlife And Festivals In Spain 82

Chapter 8: Souvenirs And Shopping in Spain 88

Souvenirs 90

Chapter 9: Tips For Traveling in Spain 94

Time-Saving Tips: 94
Money-Saving Tips: 95

Conclusion 97

Introduction

Greetings, spirit of adventure! If Germany's undulating landscapes, fascinating history, and vibrant culture have captured your attention, give yourself permission to be enthralled by another European treasure: Spain. Spain is a tapestry of history, culture, and scenic beauty, much like Germany and other European nations, but with a distinct flair and rhythm that is sure to enthrall your senses.

Imagine yourself meandering through the colorful streets of Barcelona, where the rhythmic sounds of flamenco reverberate from secret courtyards and the fanciful architecture of Gaudí meets. Or maybe you're drawn to the golden sands and blue waters of the Costa del Sol's sun-kissed beaches, where you can relax and appreciate the Mediterranean way of life. Spain provides a diverse range of experiences that cater to the interests of all types of travelers, from the grand heights of the Sierra Nevada to the lively plazas of Madrid.

You may question, though, why you would need a travel guide for Spain. Although spontaneity can be endearing, it might be intimidating to navigate Seville's maze-like streets or understand the complex history of the Alhambra without the right assistance. Your tour guide to Spain acts as a compass, pointing out hidden gems, giving background information, and making sure you have genuine, above-average experiences. A travel book becomes your trusted companion, regardless of your interests—history buffs eager to learn about Spain's colorful past, foodies keen to sample tapas and paella in neighborhood hangouts, or adventurers looking for experiences off the beaten route.

So, my dear traveler, let curiosity be your guide and Spain's entrancing appeal your muse as you stand on the precipice of a Spanish journey. Savor the delicious food, warm company, and let the soul be stirred by the beat of flamenco. When you go to Spain armed with a travel guide, you're not simply going to a place; you're going on an exploration voyage where each new chapter in Spain's enduring tale is revealed at every turn. ¡Welcome to Spain! Greetings from Spain!

Chapter 1:
Travel Essentials

A trip to Spain from Germany, or anywhere in Europe, requires careful planning and a thrilling mix of anticipation. This thorough guide will assist you in making the most of your preparations:

Best time to visit.

The ideal time to travel from Germany and throughout Europe to Spain will primarily depend on your interests, since each season has its own advantages and things to take into account. Here's a summary to assist you in making decisions depending on crowds, prices, and seasons:

1. Spring (March to May):

- **Weather**: Temperate weather is perfect for touring cities and outdoor activities without the extreme heat, especially from April onwards.
- **Cost**: Spring is regarded as shoulder season since it offers comparatively cheaper airfares and hotel rates than the busiest summer months.

- **Crowds**: Although popular towns and attractions may see an uptick in visitors during the Easter holidays, crowds are often manageable.

2. Summer (June to August):

- **Weather**: Warm to hot weather are common, particularly in Andalusia and other central and southern regions. The cool breezes of the coast are pleasant.
- **Cost**: Since summer is the busiest travel season, costs for lodging, airfare, and attractions will rise. Still, getting a reservation in advance can help you get a better deal.
- **Crowds**: Anticipate greater crowds, particularly in well-known travel locations like Barcelona, Madrid, and the Costa del Sol. To avoid peak hours, schedule your trip to the main sites for later in the afternoon or early in the morning.

3. Autumn (September to November):

- **Weather**: September and October are good months to visit because to their mild weather. November marks the beginning of a drop in temperature, particularly in the north.
- **Cost**: Similar to spring, autumn is shoulder season, offering competitive prices for accommodations and fewer crowds compared to summer.
- **Crowds**: While crowds taper off after the peak summer season, popular cities and attractions might still experience moderate tourist traffic, particularly during local festivals.

4. Winter (December to February):

- **Weather**: Winter brings cooler temperatures, especially in central and northern regions, with potential snowfall in mountainous areas like the Sierra Nevada.
- **Cost**: Winter is off-peak season, offering the lowest prices

for accommodations, flights, and attractions. You'll find great deals on hotels and fewer crowds at major tourist sites.
- **Crowds**: With the exception of Christmas and New Year's holidays, Spain experiences fewer tourists during winter, making it an excellent time to explore popular cities without the crowds.

Recommendations:

- **Festivals and Events**: Before you plan your trip to Spain, think about the exciting festival schedule. Worldwide visitors are drawn to events such as Semana Santa (Holy Week), Feria de Abril in Seville, and La Tomatina in Buñol, which could impact the dates you choose to vacation.
- **Region-Specific**: Spain's diverse geography means that weather patterns can vary significantly between regions. Coastal areas like Andalusia and Catalonia experience milder winters, while northern regions like Basque Country and Galicia can be cooler and wetter.
- **Personal Preferences**: Consider your travel priorities, whether it's exploring historical sites, enjoying beach holidays, or experiencing local festivals. Aligning your travel dates with your interests will enhance your overall experience.

In conclusion, the best time to visit Spain depends on balancing your preferences for weather, budget, and crowds. Whether you're drawn to the vibrant energy of summer, the mild temperatures of spring and autumn, or the tranquility of winter, Spain awaits with its myriad of experiences and enchanting landscapes.

What to pack

When packing for a trip to Spain, keep in mind the activities you have scheduled, the time of year, and your own preferences. Here is a thorough packing list to assist you in getting ready for your trip:

Clothing:

1. **Seasonal Attire:**
   - **Summer:** Lightweight and breathable clothing, including shorts, T-shirts, sundresses, and swimwear (if visiting coastal areas).
   - **Spring & Autumn:** Layered clothing for varying temperatures, including light jackets, long-sleeved shirts, jeans, and comfortable walking shoes.
   - **Winter:** Warm clothing, including sweaters, coats, scarves, gloves, and waterproof footwear, especially if visiting northern regions.
2. **Footwear:**
   - Comfortable walking shoes for exploring cities and attractions.
   - Sandals or breathable shoes for warmer weather.
   - Waterproof or insulated boots for winter or outdoor activities.
3. **Accessories:**
   - Sunhat, sunglasses, and sunscreen for protection against UV rays.
   - Umbrella or compact rain jacket for unexpected showers.
   - Swimwear and beach towel for coastal regions or hotel pools.

Travel Essentials:

1. **Documentation:**
   - Passport, visa (if required), and travel insurance details.
   - Photocopies of important documents stored separately.
   - Printed or digital copies of hotel reservations, transportation tickets, and itinerary.
2. **Technology:**

- Smartphone, charger, and portable power bank.
- Camera or smartphone for capturing memories.
- Universal adapter to charge electronic devices.
- Headphones or earbuds for entertainment during travel.

3. **Personal Items**:
   - Toiletries, including toothbrush, toothpaste, shampoo, conditioner, and skincare products in travel-sized containers.
   - Personal medications, prescriptions, and a basic first-aid kit.
   - Travel-sized hand sanitizer and disinfectant wipes.

Miscellaneous Items:

1. **Travel Accessories**:
   - Lightweight travel backpack or daypack for daily excursions.
   - Luggage locks or TSA-approved locks for added security.
   - Travel pillow and eye mask for comfort during long flights or train journeys.
2. **Language & Navigation**:
   - Pocket-sized Spanish phrasebook or language translation app.
   - Maps, guidebooks, or digital travel apps for navigating cities and attractions.
   - Printed or digital reservations for activities, tours, and restaurants.
3. **Snacks & Refreshments**:
   - Reusable water bottle to stay hydrated.
   - Snacks like granola bars, nuts, or dried fruits for on-the-go energy.

Final Tips:

- **Pack Light**: Opt for versatile clothing items that can be mixed and matched to create multiple outfits. Consider packing clothing made from moisture-wicking and quick-drying materials, especially for summer travel.
- **Check Airline Restrictions**: If flying, review airline baggage policies regarding weight limits, carry-on restrictions, and additional fees.
- **Local Considerations**: Familiarize yourself with Spain's cultural norms and dress codes, especially when visiting religious sites or participating in specific events or activities.

Getting there and moving around

- Navigating from Germany to Spain and moving around within the country involves a range of transportation options tailored to your preferences, budget, and itinerary. Here's a detailed guide to help you plan your journey and explore Spain seamlessly:

Getting There:

- **Flights**:
- **Direct Flights**: Major airports in Germany, such as Frankfurt, Berlin, Munich, and Düsseldorf, offer direct flights to primary Spanish cities, including Madrid, Barcelona, Valencia, Seville, and Málaga. Airlines such as Lufthansa, Iberia, Ryanair, and Vueling operate frequent routes between Germany and Spain.
- **Flight Duration**: The flight duration from Germany to Spain typically ranges from 2 to 3 hours, depending on the departure and arrival cities.
- **Rail**:
- **High-Speed Trains (AVE)**: Spain's high-speed rail network, operated by Renfe, connects major cities like Madrid,

Barcelona, Seville, Valencia, and Málaga. Consider purchasing advance tickets for AVE trains to secure lower fares and preferred seating options.
- **Eurail Pass**: If you're exploring multiple European countries, consider purchasing a Eurail Pass, which offers flexible travel options and access to Spain's high-speed rail network.
- **Road**:
- **Driving**: If you prefer a scenic road trip, consider renting a car in Germany and driving to Spain. The journey offers picturesque landscapes, especially when crossing the French-Spanish border via the Pyrenees Mountains. Ensure you have the necessary international driving permits, insurance coverage, and familiarize yourself with Spain's traffic rules and regulations.

Moving Around in Spain:

- **Public Transportation**:
- **Metro & Buses**: Major cities like Madrid, Barcelona, Valencia, and Seville offer efficient metro systems, trams, and bus networks for navigating urban areas. Purchase multi-trip tickets or travel cards for cost-effective transportation options.
- **Local Trains**: Regional trains and commuter services connect cities, towns, and scenic regions within Spain. Renfe operates various train services, including Cercanías (commuter trains) and regional express trains.
- **Inter-City Transport**:
- **High-Speed Trains (AVE)**: Travel between major cities quickly and comfortably using Spain's AVE high-speed trains. Book tickets in advance to benefit from promotional fares and seat selection options.
- **Long-Distance Buses**: Consider traveling by long-distance buses operated by companies like ALSA and FlixBus, offering affordable fares and extensive route networks

across Spain.
- **Car Rentals & Driving:**
- **Renting a Car:** Renting a car provides flexibility, especially when exploring rural areas, coastal regions, and off-the-beaten-path destinations. Major car rental companies operate in Spain, offering a range of vehicles to suit your travel needs.
- **Road Network:** Spain boasts a well-maintained road network, including highways (autopistas) and secondary roads (carreteras), connecting cities, towns, and tourist destinations. Ensure you have updated maps, GPS navigation, and adhere to speed limits and traffic regulations.
- **Travel Tips:**
- **Planning & Reservations:** Research transportation options, schedules, and fares in advance, especially during peak tourist seasons or holidays. Booking tickets and making reservations ahead of time can help secure preferred travel times and seats.
- **Travel Apps & Resources:** Utilize travel apps, websites, and resources to compare transportation options, access real-time schedules, and receive updates on route changes or disruptions.
- **Local Insights & Recommendations:** Engage with locals, hotel staff, and tourism offices for personalized recommendations, travel tips, and insights on navigating Spain's diverse regions and attractions.

1. **Official Language:**
   - **Spanish (Castilian):** Spanish, commonly referred to as Castilian (Castellano), is the official language of Spain and widely spoken throughout the country. While regional languages such as Catalan, Galician, and Basque coexist alongside Spanish, you'll find that most

Spaniards are fluent in Castilian.
2. **Regional Languages**:
   - **Catalan**: Spoken predominantly in Catalonia, including Barcelona and Girona.
   - **Galician**: Commonly spoken in Galicia, particularly in cities like Santiago de Compostela and Vigo.
   - **Basque (Euskara)**: Native to the Basque Country, including cities like Bilbao and San Sebastián.

Communication Tips & Resources:

1. **Basic Spanish Phrases**:
   - **Greetings**: Learn essential phrases such as "Hola" (Hello), "Buenos días" (Good morning), "Por favor" (Please), and "Gracias" (Thank you) to initiate conversations and show courtesy.
   - **Navigational Phrases**: Familiarize yourself with phrases like "¿Dónde está...?" (Where is...?), "¿Cuánto cuesta?" (How much does it cost?), and "Necesito ayuda" (I need help) to seek information, directions, or assistance.
2. **Language Apps & Resources**:
   - **Translation Apps**: Utilize language translation apps such as Google Translate, Duolingo, or iTranslate for real-time translations, voice recognition, and offline capabilities. These apps can assist with translating menus, signs, conversations, and essential information during your travels.
   - **Phrasebooks & Guides**: Carry a pocket-sized Spanish phrasebook or travel guide featuring common phrases, expressions, and cultural insights to facilitate communication and immerse yourself in Spain's linguistic and cultural nuances.
3. **Engage & Practice**:
   - **Local Interactions**: Engage with locals, hotel staff, restaurant servers, and fellow travelers to practice your

Spanish, ask questions, and receive personalized recommendations. Spaniards appreciate efforts to communicate in their language and often respond warmly to genuine attempts to converse in Spanish.
- **Language Exchange**: Consider participating in language exchange events, workshops, or online platforms to practice Spanish, meet local residents, and gain insights into Spain's diverse cultures, traditions, and regions.

Cultural Considerations:

1. **Dialects & Regional Variations**:
   - **Accents & Pronunciations**: Embrace regional accents, dialects, and variations in pronunciation when interacting with locals across Spain. While Castilian Spanish serves as the standard language, each region offers unique linguistic features, expressions, and cultural nuances that enrich your travel experience.
2. **Respect & Courtesy:**
   - **Politeness & Etiquette**: Show respect and courtesy towards locals by using formal greetings, addressing individuals appropriately (e.g., "Señor" for Mr., "Señora" for Mrs.), and demonstrating cultural awareness and sensitivity during conversations and interactions.

Final Thoughts:

Embracing Spain's linguistic diversity, engaging with locals, and immersing yourself in the language and culture enhance your travel experience, foster connections, and create memorable moments throughout your journey. By learning basic Spanish phrases, utilizing language resources, and appreciating regional variations, you'll navigate Spain's vibrant cities, picturesque landscapes, and rich cultural heritage with confidence, curiosity, and enthusiasm. ¡Buena suerte y disfruta de tu viaje! Good luck and enjoy your trip!

You

language information for travellers to spain

1 / 3

ChatGPT

Practical information

Language

Navigating the language landscape as a traveler to Spain requires a blend of linguistic awareness, cultural sensitivity, and practical communication skills. Here's a tailored guide to help you engage, communicate, and immerse yourself in Spain's rich linguistic and cultural tapestry:

Language Overview:

1. **Official Language**:
    - **Spanish (Castilian)**: Spanish, known as Castilian (Castellano), serves as the official language of Spain. While you'll encounter regional languages and dialects, Castilian remains the predominant language spoken across the country.
2. **Regional Languages & Dialects**:
    - **Catalan**: Spoken primarily in Catalonia, including cities like Barcelona and Tarragona. Catalan shares similarities with Spanish but boasts distinct linguistic features, expressions, and cultural nuances.
    - **Galician**: Native to Galicia, particularly in cities such as Santiago de Compostela and Vigo. Galician bears similarities to Portuguese and features unique linguistic

characteristics reflecting the region's Celtic heritage.
- **Basque (Euskara)**: Unique to the Basque Country, including cities like Bilbao and San Sebastián. Basque remains a linguistic mystery with no known linguistic connections to other languages, offering a distinctive cultural and linguistic experience.

Practical Communication Tips:

1. **Essential Phrases & Expressions**:
    - **Greetings & Courtesies**: Learn fundamental phrases such as "Hola" (Hello), "Buenos días" (Good morning), "Por favor" (Please), "Gracias" (Thank you), and "¿Cómo estás?" (How are you?) to initiate conversations, show respect, and engage with locals.
    - **Navigational & Transactional Phrases**: Familiarize yourself with phrases like "¿Dónde está...?" (Where is...?), "¿Cuánto cuesta?" (How much does it cost?), "Necesito ayuda" (I need help), and "La cuenta, por favor" (The bill, please) to seek information, directions, or assistance during your travels.
2. **Language Apps & Resources**:
    - **Translation Tools**: Utilize language translation apps such as Google Translate, Duolingo, or iTranslate for on-the-go translations, voice recognition, and offline capabilities. These tools assist with deciphering menus, signs, conversations, and essential information while exploring Spain.
    - **Phrasebooks & Guides**: Carry a pocket-sized Spanish phrasebook or travel guide featuring common phrases, expressions, and cultural insights to facilitate communication, enhance interactions, and immerse yourself in Spain's diverse linguistic landscape.
3. **Engage & Interact**:
    - **Local Encounters**: Embrace opportunities to engage with locals, hotel staff, restaurant servers, and fellow

travelers in Spanish. Demonstrating efforts to communicate, practicing basic phrases, and expressing genuine interest in Spain's language and culture fosters connections, enriches experiences, and creates memorable moments throughout your journey.

Cultural Considerations:

1. **Dialectal Variations & Regional Nuances:**
   - **Accents & Pronunciations:** Embrace regional accents, dialects, and variations in pronunciation when interacting with locals across Spain. Each region offers unique linguistic features, expressions, and cultural nuances that reflect Spain's diverse heritage, history, and identity.
2. **Respect & Cultural Sensitivity:**
   - **Politeness & Etiquette:** Show respect and courtesy towards locals by using formal greetings, addressing individuals appropriately, and demonstrating cultural awareness during conversations and interactions. Recognizing regional differences, embracing linguistic diversity, and adapting to local customs and traditions enhance your travel experience and foster meaningful connections with Spaniards.

Currency and banking Navigating currency and banking as a traveler from Germany to Spain involves understanding Spain's financial landscape, currency, banking facilities, and essential considerations to manage your finances effectively during your journey. Here's a comprehensive guide to help you prepare for your travels:

Currency Overview:

1. **Official Currency:**
   - **Euro (€):** Spain's official currency is the Euro (€),

denoted by the symbol "€." The Euro is widely accepted across Spain, including major cities, tourist destinations, hotels, restaurants, and retail establishments.

Banking & Financial Facilities:

1. **ATMs & Cash Withdrawals:**
   - **Availability**: ATMs (Cajeros automáticos) are widely available throughout Spain, especially in urban areas, airports, train stations, shopping centers, and tourist destinations. Major banks in Spain include Banco Santander, BBVA, CaixaBank, and Banco Sabadell.
   - **International Cards**: Ensure your debit and credit cards are enabled for international transactions and notify your bank of your travel dates to Spain to avoid any potential card blockages or security alerts.
   - **ATM Fees**: Be aware of potential ATM fees, including foreign transaction fees, currency conversion fees, and service charges imposed by your home bank and the local Spanish bank. Consider withdrawing larger amounts less frequently to minimize fees and secure favorable exchange rates.
2. **Currency Exchange:**
   - **Exchange Offices**: Currency exchange offices (Casas de Cambio) are available in major cities, airports, and tourist areas. While convenient, these establishments may offer less favorable exchange rates and higher fees compared to withdrawing cash from ATMs or using credit cards.
   - **Banks**: Consider exchanging currency at reputable banks or financial institutions in Spain for competitive rates, transparent fees, and reliable services. Compare exchange rates, inquire about fees, and review terms and conditions before completing transactions.
3. **Credit Cards & Payments:**
   - **Acceptance**: Major credit cards, including Visa,

Mastercard, American Express, and Diners Club, are widely accepted in Spain, especially in urban areas, hotels, restaurants, and retail establishments. However, always carry cash for smaller vendors, markets, and establishments that may not accept credit cards.
- **Contactless Payments**: Utilize contactless payments, mobile wallets (e.g., Apple Pay, Google Pay), and chip-and-PIN technology prevalent in Spain to facilitate secure and convenient transactions during your travels.

Traveler's Tips & Recommendations:

1. **Currency Conversion & Exchange Rates**:
   - **Real-time Rates**: Monitor currency conversion rates, exchange rate fluctuations, and market trends using reputable financial websites, mobile apps, or currency conversion tools to assess the best times to exchange currency, withdraw cash, or make payments in Spain.
2. **Banking Hours & Accessibility**:
   - **Operating Hours**: Familiarize yourself with Spanish banking hours, which typically operate from Monday to Friday, 9:00 AM to 2:00 PM, with limited hours on Saturdays. Plan your banking transactions, cash withdrawals, and financial activities accordingly to avoid inconvenience or delays during your travels.
3. **Safety & Security**:
   - **Financial Precautions**: Safeguard your debit and credit cards, avoid displaying large amounts of cash, and maintain vigilant awareness of your surroundings to mitigate the risk of theft, fraud, or unauthorized transactions during your travels in Spain.
   - **Emergency Contacts**: Keep a record of your bank's emergency contact information, customer service hotline, and card replacement services in case of lost or stolen cards, unauthorized transactions, or financial emergencies while traveling.

Safety

Safety is paramount when traveling, and while Spain is generally considered a safe destination for tourists, it's essential to remain vigilant and informed to ensure a pleasant and secure experience. Here's a comprehensive guide outlining safety information for travelers to Spain:

General Safety Tips:

1. **Awareness & Vigilance:**
   - **Tourist Areas:** Exercise caution in crowded tourist areas, airports, train stations, and popular attractions, where pickpocketing, theft, and scams may occur. Remain vigilant, especially during peak tourist seasons and major events or festivals.
   - **Street Safety:** Be aware of your surroundings, avoid displaying valuables (e.g., expensive jewelry, cameras, smartphones), and secure personal belongings in zippered compartments or cross-body bags to deter opportunistic theft.
2. **Travel Documents & Personal Identification:**
   - **Secure Documents:** Safeguard your passport, identification, travel insurance details, and other essential documents in a secure location, such as a hotel safe deposit box. Carry photocopies or digital copies of travel documents and maintain contact information for the nearest embassy or consulate.
3. **Emergency Contacts & Communication:**
   - **Emergency Numbers:** Familiarize yourself with Spain's emergency contact numbers, including:
     - Police: 112
     - Ambulance: 112
     - Fire Department: 112
   - **Local Authorities:** Report incidents, thefts, or emergencies to local police or tourist information offices

promptly. Maintain a list of essential contacts, including your hotel, tour operators, and emergency services, for immediate assistance.

Specific Safety Considerations:

1. **Transportation Safety**:
   - **Public Transport**: Utilize reputable and licensed transportation services, including taxis, buses, trains, and metro systems, especially during nighttime hours. Verify official identification, use designated taxi stands, and avoid unlicensed or unauthorized transportation services.
   - **Driving**: If renting a car or driving in Spain, adhere to local traffic laws, regulations, and speed limits. Familiarize yourself with road signs, signals, and parking restrictions to navigate safely and avoid potential fines or penalties.
2. **Health & Wellness**:
   - **Medical Emergencies**: Seek medical attention promptly for injuries, illnesses, or health-related concerns. Ensure you have adequate travel insurance coverage, familiarize yourself with Spain's healthcare system, and carry essential medications, prescriptions, and a basic first-aid kit.
   - **Water & Food Safety**: Consume bottled or filtered water and exercise caution when consuming street food, seafood, or unpasteurized dairy products to minimize the risk of foodborne illnesses or gastrointestinal issues.
3. **Natural Disasters & Environmental Considerations**:
   - **Weather Awareness**: Monitor local weather forecasts, advisories, and seasonal patterns to prepare for potential weather-related hazards, including heatwaves, storms, wildfires, or flooding. Follow local authorities' instructions, stay informed, and seek shelter or evacuation if necessary.

- **Outdoor Activities**: Exercise caution when engaging in outdoor activities, water sports, or adventure tourism. Consult local guides, tour operators, and official sources for safety guidelines, equipment requirements, and potential risks associated with specific activities or regions.

Cultural & Social Considerations:

1. **Respect & Etiquette**:
   - **Cultural Sensitivity**: Respect Spain's cultural norms, traditions, customs, and social etiquette. Familiarize yourself with local customs, gestures, dress codes, and behaviors to interact respectfully with residents, especially in religious, historical, or traditional settings.
   - **Public Behavior**: Maintain decorum, avoid disruptive or disrespectful behaviors, and adhere to local laws, regulations, and guidelines governing public conduct, alcohol consumption, and social interactions in Spain.

Final Thoughts:

By prioritizing safety, maintaining awareness, and exercising caution, you'll enjoy a secure, enriching, and memorable travel experience in Spain. Embrace the country's diverse landscapes, vibrant cultures, and warm hospitality while safeguarding your well-being and respecting local communities. ¡Viaje seguro y disfrute de España! Safe travels and enjoy Spain!

You

ten reasons why you as a GERMAN MUST VISIT SPAIN

ChatGPT

ChatGPT

Certainly! Here are ten compelling reasons why a German should consider visiting Spain:

1. **Cultural Richness**: Spain boasts a diverse cultural heritage influenced by various civilizations, including the Romans, Moors, and Catholic monarchs. Experience this richness through its architecture, traditions, festivals, and arts.
2. **Culinary Delights**: Indulge in Spain's world-renowned cuisine, from savory paellas and tapas to delectable jamón ibérico, wines, and cheeses. Savor the authentic flavors, regional specialties, and gastronomic traditions that tantalize the palate.
3. **Stunning Landscapes**: Explore Spain's breathtaking landscapes, from the sun-drenched beaches of Costa del Sol and Balearic Islands to the majestic peaks of the Pyrenees Mountains, verdant valleys, and picturesque countryside.
4. **Vibrant Cities**: Discover Spain's vibrant cities, including Madrid, Barcelona, Seville, Valencia, and Bilbao, each offering unique attractions, architectural marvels, cultural landmarks, and bustling urban environments.
5. **Historical Sites**: Immerse yourself in Spain's rich history by visiting UNESCO World Heritage sites such as the Alhambra in Granada, Sagrada Familia in Barcelona, Toledo's historic city center, and Segovia's Roman aqueduct.
6. **Artistic Legacy**: Experience Spain's artistic legacy through its world-renowned museums, galleries, and landmarks, including the Prado Museum in Madrid, Guggenheim Museum in Bilbao, Picasso Museum in Barcelona, and Salvador Dalí's Theatre-Museum in Figueres.
7. **Festivals & Celebrations**: Participate in Spain's vibrant festivals and celebrations, such as La Tomatina in Buñol, Feria de Abril in Seville, San Fermín in Pamplona, and Semana Santa (Holy Week) events across the country.
8. **Outdoor Activities**: Engage in a range of outdoor activities and adventures, including hiking in the Sierra Nevada,

skiing in the Pyrenees, surfing in Tarifa, cycling along the Camino de Santiago, and exploring Spain's natural parks, reserves, and coastal regions.
9. **Warm Hospitality**: Experience Spain's warm and welcoming hospitality, characterized by the friendly demeanor, generosity, and passion of its people. Engage with locals, immerse yourself in the local culture, and forge meaningful connections that enhance your travel experience.
10. **Linguistic & Cultural Connection**: Deepen your understanding and appreciation of the Spanish language, culture, and traditions by immersing yourself in Spain's diverse regions, languages, dialects, and historical influences. Embrace the opportunity to learn, grow, and expand your horizons while exploring Spain's captivating landscapes and vibrant communities.

Chapter 2:
Must Visit Places in Spain

Here are ten compelling reasons why a German and any European should consider visiting Spain:

1. Cultural Richness:

Spain's festivals, music, dance, and architecture all reflect the country's diverse cultural heritage. Spain's rich cultural environment reflects Germany's rich history, from the fine features of Moorish architecture in Andalusia to the Gothic grandeur of Barcelona's cathedrals. Discover regional customs, historical places, and UNESCO World Heritage sites that highlight Spain's distinct identity and ties to Europe.

2. Culinary Delights:

Spanish cuisine is known for its bright flavors, use of fresh ingredients, and regional delicacies that fascinate the senses. Savor delicious paellas, mouthwatering seafood dishes, real tapas, and premium wines from well-known areas like Priorat, Rioja, and Ribera del Duero. Discover gastronomy festivals, local markets, cooking workshops, and culinary traditions that honor Spain's inventiveness and rich culinary legacy.

3. Stunning Landscapes:

Due to its varied topography, Spain is home to a wide variety of landscapes, including snow-capped mountains, lush forests, attractive valleys, and sun-kissed beaches and rocky coastlines. Discover the adventure, leisure, and discovery options offered by Spain's natural parks, reserves, and outdoor attractions, such as the Canary Islands, Balearic Islands, Picos de Europa, Camino de Santiago, and Costa Brava.

4. Vibrant Cities:

Spain's dynamic cities enthrall tourists with their urban experiences, cultural attractions, and dynamic energy. Explore the artistic boulevards of Madrid, the architectural marvels of Barcelona, the ancient appeal of Seville, the futuristic allure of Valencia, and the cultural resurgence of Bilbao. Experience Spain's vibrant cities, vibrant nightlife, upscale malls, and well-known sites that highlight the nation's modernism, inventiveness, and worldwide influence.

5. Historical Sites:

Roman ruins, mediaeval castles, archaeological sites, and famous landmarks all contribute to the rich history of Spain. Experience the historical legacy, architectural wonders, and UNESCO World Heritage sites of Spain by visiting the Alhambra in Granada, the Cathedral of Santiago de Compostela, the Roman aqueduct in Segovia, and the old city of Tarragona.

6. Artistic Legacy:

Spain has a rich cultural heritage spanning centuries of inventiveness, creativity, and expression. Discover internationally recognized art sites, galleries, and museums, such as the Thyssen-Bornemisza Museum, the Guggenheim Museum Bilbao, the Prado Museum, the Reina Sofia Museum, and Salvador Dalí's bizarre works. Take part in the dynamic cultural communities, modern art scene, and artistic legacy of Spain to enthrall and inspire tourists.

7. Festivals & Celebrations:

Spain's colorful festivals and celebrations highlight the country's customs, diversity of culture, and sense of community. Take part in well-known celebrations like La Tomatina, Pamplona's Running of the Bulls, Feria de Abril, Tenerife's Carnival, and Semana Santa to get a taste of Spain's joyous vibe, music, dancing, and regional customs that bring people together to celebrate.

8. Outdoor Activities:

The varied topography of Spain is a nature lover's and outdoor enthusiast's dream come true. Explore Spain's natural parks, coastal areas, mountains, and islands with hiking, cycling, skiing, water sports, birdwatching, and ecotourism activities. Discover the outdoor attractions, adventure travel options, and eco-friendly travel programs in Spain that support environmental education, conservation, and appreciation.

9. Warm Hospitality:

Germans who are looking for real experiences, relationships, and cultural immersion are drawn to Spain's friendly and inviting hospitality. Stay at family-run lodgings (such as paradores or rustic guesthouses), mingle with people, take part in local events, and embrace Spain's culture of hospitality, companionship, and shared experiences that create enduring memories and friendships.

10. Linguistic & Cultural Connection:

Accept the linguistic variety, cultural customs, and regional identities of Spain to increase your understanding of the ties and common history of Europe. Study Spanish, converse in regional tongues (such as Catalan, Galician, and Basque), take part in cultural exchanges, and discover the various regions, customs, holidays, and historical influences of Spain that honor diversity, cooperation, and European unity.

These are the top ten places in Spain that you simply must see.

1. Barcelona

Barcelona is well-known for Antoni Gaudi's magnificent architectural creations. In his works, he has a distinct and individualistic style. His extravagant and spectacular buildings in Barcelona have grown to become the main draws for visitors. Because Gaudi was a practitioner of Catalan Modernism, Barcelona is frequently referred to as the Catalan city. Among the noteworthy mentions are his landmark "The Sagrada Familia Church," "Casa Mila," "Picasso Museum," "Casa Batllo," and "Parc Güell." Barcelona is without a doubt among the world's top tourism destinations. It also serves as home to the famous Barcelona Football Club. The energetic seaside city is well-known for its fantastic food selections, exciting shopping arcades, and exciting nightlife.

2. **Madrid**

In the center of Spain is the historic city of Madrid. Madrid, the capital of Spain, is a well-known travel destination full of surprises. You'll be amazed by the best museums and artwork in the world, mouthwatering dining options, a bustling nightlife, pedestrian zones full of stores, cafes, and restaurants, and amazing architectural feats. Madrid is renowned for its rich creative and cultural legacy because of its more than 70 institutions, which include the Prado Museum, the Thyssen-Bornemisza Museum, and the Reina Sofia National Art Center. Madrid exudes internationalism, experience, and sophistication. One of the world's top sports teams, Real Madrid Football Club, is based in Madrid.

3. Granada

Situated at the foot of the stunning Sierra Nevada Mountain range in Spain, Granada boasts a rich history and customs. It acts as Granada's regional capital. The area is renowned for the stunning fusion of nightlife, traditions, and culture, in addition to the attractiveness of the world-famous Alhambra. The Alhambra complex from the Middle Ages is a magnificent example of medieval architecture. Moorish poets referred to it as "a pearl studded in emeralds" and it is now recognized as a World Heritage Site. It was remodeled into a palace after being constructed as a fort initially. The spectacular Alhambra complex features geometric elements mixed with Arabic calligraphy and engravings. It is crowned with tranquil gardens with well-planned trees, flowers, and courtyards as well as paths for wandering. There are a lot of historic homes, churches, and mosques, and the views of the city below are breathtaking.

4. Seville

Andalusia's capital, Sevilla, is the fourth-biggest city in Spain. There are three World Heritage Sites in Seville. These are the Santa Maria de la Sede Cathedral, the Reales Alcázares Palace, and the General Archive of the Indies, which is home to Christopher Columbus's bones. It acts as the region's center of commerce and culture. Apart from its impressive architectural features, the location provides a lively nightlife and events. Tourist numbers are high during major celebrations like "Semana Santa" and "Feria de Abril." The orange blossom scent and the city of Seville's brilliant, vivid colors will captivate your senses.

5. Bilbao

Bilbao is the gateway to Spain and the center of Basque customs, culture, and artistic expression. It is a significant port city in Northern Spain that is fast growing as an urban area. Bilbao offers a different perspective on traditional art. Bilbao's modern architecture sets it apart from other Spanish places. In the historic port city, "The Guggenheim Museum" is the most popular destination. It was designed by Frank Gehry in 1997. The museum is housed in a cutting-edge titanium building that features modern and contemporary art.

6. Valencia

The impressive, cutting-edge structures that make Valencia the "City of Arts and Sciences" include the Oceanarium, Planetarium, and Interactive Museum. Another theory holds that the paella originated in Valencia. This place is a masterful fusion of the contemporary and the historic. There are a lot of sports facilities in the city that are beautifully encircled by greenery, including trees and plants. The beach adds to the charm as well. Valencia hosts the Fallas Festival in March, during which papier-mâché figures in a variety of hues and forms are on display. At the end of the same week, the figures are ceremoniously burned, and the towns celebrate all night long.

7. Burgos

Another moniker for Burgos City is the Land of Castles. The charming city reflects its medieval origins. Situated on the banks of the Arlanza and Duero rivers, Burgos is a historical treasure in Spain. The Cathedral of Burgos has been inducted as a World Heritage Site by UNESCO. The region has a distinct northern Castilian vibe and is home to a few scattered medieval ruins, like the Abbey of Santa Maria la Real de Las Huelgas and the Cartuja de Miraflores. Burgos is a tidy, tranquil city. It is welcome and encouraged for visitors to stroll around the city to take in more of its breathtaking scenery.

8. Corboda

Originally built by the Romans, Cordoba was a harbor city on the Guadalquivir River. It later became the capital city of Al-Andalus, the Moorish empire that controlled Islamic Spain. Corboda is among the most picturesque cities in Spain. It's a great place to explore on foot or by bicycle. The primary attraction is unquestionably the fascinating Mezquita, one of the largest and most famous Islamic buildings in the world. There's even a cathedral built in the midst of all the columns and arches. The imaginative patios and courtyards decorated with a rainbow of colorful flowers are breathtaking!

9. Segovia

As a World Heritage City, Segovia is home to numerous, outstanding monuments and buildings that draw large crowds of tourists. But Segovia has a lot more to offer. An elegant residential neighborhood, a historic Jewish neighborhood, picturesque scenery, and a green space provide for the perfect daytime stroll in the sun. Located to the north of Madrid is this charming city. It was founded, so the story goes, by Hercules or Noah's son. The city provided inspiration for Walt Disney's Sleeping Beauty's castle. These are good enough reasons to include this location on your bucket list.

10. Spanish Islands

Spain is home to some of the most beautiful islands in Europe. About equal parts of the main Spanish islands are made up of the Balearic Islands and the Canary Islands. Located east of the Spanish peninsula, the four main Balearic Islands are Ibiza, Formentera, Mallorca, and Minorca. Each island has its own unique character from the rest of the country. Mallorca is the largest and most popular Balearic Island, whereas Ibiza is well-known for being a party island. The Canary Islands, or simply the Canaries, are located in the Atlantic Ocean just off the coast of Morocco's southern region. Two of its most significant natural attractions are the Teide Volcano in Tenerife and the Maspalomas Dunes in Gran Canaria. Along with other notable qualities, they are also well recognized for having wonderful beaches and a pleasant, moderate temperature. "La Palma," "Gran Canaria," "Lanzarote," and "La Gomera" are some of the most beautiful and well-known Spanish islands.

Famous Architectural Wonders to Visit in Spain

Some of the most innovative modern architectural movements originated in Spain. From pre-Romanesque to Gothic Spanish architecture, Spain has some of the outstanding specimens of the genre. The most well-known modern and contemporary Spanish architect, Antoni Gaudí, is renowned for his incredible building designs. Many Spanish architects are currently pushing the limits of modern design and creating some of the most avant-garde forms.

1. City of Arts and Science

The City of Arts and Scientific in Valencia is a cultural complex featuring an outdoor aquarium, a scientific museum, and an IMAX theater. It is recognized as one of Spain's twelve treasures. It is thought to be the biggest and most contentious of Calatrava's creations. A major tourist site, this entertainment-focused cultural and architectural complex is one of Spain's most magnificent buildings.

2. Metropol Parasol

Designed by renowned German architect Jürgen Mayer, this gorgeous wooden building is situated in Seville's old neighborhood. With a height of 26 meters, it is considered the largest wooden construction in the world. This extraordinary piece of art is commonly known as Las Setas de la Encarnacion. Inspired by the Seville Cathedral's vaults, this construction is made up of six parasols that resemble enormous mushrooms.

3. Guggenheim Museum

The Guggenheim Museum, a modern art museum, was designed by Canadian-American architect Frank Gerry and is located close to the Nervion River. Located in Bilbao, Spain, King Juan Carlos inaugurated this museum's doors in 1997. This remarkable example of modern architecture has garnered admiration from a wide audience. Some observers have even gone so far as to call it one of those special landmarks in the world.

4. Torre Glories

Torre Glories is one of Barcelona's most famous monuments. Jean Novel, a French architect, designed this 38-story building. The real address or headquarters of Barcelona's water utility are located between Avinguda Diagonal and Carrer Badajoz. The Agbar Group, the proprietors of the water utility, are honored by having this skyscraper called the Torre Agbar.

5. Bridge Pavilion

One of the most famous buildings in Spain is the Bridge Pavilion, which was created by British-Iraqi architect Zahra Hadis. Approximately 10,000 visitors per hour are typically anticipated to visit the Pavilion during the global exhibition. This creative 280-meter bridge spans the Ebro River and links the La Almozara area. This magnificent glass bridge spans the Ebro River and passes over the capital of Aragon.

6. Oscar Niemeyer International Cultural Centre

This international project was designed by the well-known Brazilian architect Oscar Niemeyer. Located on the Aviles Estuary lies the Oscar Niemeyer International Cultural Centre, also commonly known as El Niemeyer. Its unusual exterior color scheme of red, yellow, and white makes it a prominent element in the town's scenery. One of this building's most appealing features is its massive size.

5. Hotel Marques de Riscal

It's a great idea to begin your Spanish trip at this stunning hotel. Frank Gehry combined sandstone blocks with pink titanium and gold metal ribbons that arched out of the vineyards to create this architectural masterpiece. The striking exterior and first-rate hotel amenities of this lovely hotel attract a lot of visitors. This is next to one of Rioja, Spain's oldest wineries, Vinos Herederos del Marques de Riscal.

6. Concert Hall

The Marine Park and the port's border are separated by the Canary Islands Concert Hall. Its concrete construction and sweeping, arched roof, which in some ways resembles a massive breaking wave, give the building a little more drama. Santiago Calatrava, a Spanish architect, created this magnificent theater.

7. Museo Del Prado

Located in the center of Madrid, this is the National Art Museum of Spain. It houses a sizable and superb collection of European art from the 12th century. One of the greatest museums in the world, the Museo Del Prado, has an extensive collection. It was originally founded as a museum specializing in paintings and sculptures, but it currently hosts a diverse collection of other pieces. The Del Prado is among the greatest and most well-known museums in the entire globe.

8. Barcelona's Sagrada Familia and Gaud Locales

Some have claimed that Antoni Gaud went above and beyond, even into madness, with the compositional style known as "Craftsmanship Nouveau." The most popular tourist attractions in Barcelona are now identifiable monuments that he designed, notwithstanding their idiosyncrasy.

The most important is the Baslica de la Sagrada Familia, also known as the Sanctuary Expiatori de la Sagrada Familia or the Sacred Family Church of the Compensation.

From the pinnacle of the chapel, you can observe the ongoing building below. It's among the most inventive chapels in all of Europe.

The last and most well-known common work of Gaud, Casa Milà, has no clear straight lines and seems more like a model building than a real structure. Make sure you ascend to the rooftop of the smokestacks, as it is said to have awakened the visage of Darth Vader from Star Wars.

Wizardry Evenings are conducted outdoors on the housetop terrace of the spectacular Casa Batlló, a renowned Gaud design with covered overhangs and a sloping façade that opened in 2022.

Perched above the city, Parc Güell is adorned with magnificent mosaics made of clay chard for its plans and nurseries, which are surrounded by octopuses, fish, and other exotic animals.

Bright ceramic tiles usually adorn a whimsically altered residence near the entryway.

There is just one clear reason why Gaud's landmarks are attractive to look at, even for adults and kids who have no interest in engineering.

9. The Incomparable Mosque of Cordoba (La Mezquita)

The largest mosque in western Islam, Cordoba's Extraordinary Mosque is still known as La Mezquita. It is one of the biggest mosques in the world and the epitome of Moorish architecture in Spain.

The Alhambra in Granada and the Incomparable Mosque are arguably the two most remarkable instances of Islamic engineering and craftsmanship in western Europe, although the latter's central Catholic church structure was later added after the mosque's midsection was demolished.

Commencing in 785, the development incorporated elements from Visigothic and Roman structures. By 1000, it had attained its present state, with a request corridor with a minimum of nineteen corridors. No matter where you stand or look, its sectional lines and modified Moorish curves align in even examples.

Some of Córdoba's other main tourist destinations are the Alcázar de los Reyes Cristianos, the former Caliphal Castle that Catholic lord Fernando III took over in the thirteenth century, the Palacio de Viana, a fifteenth-century noble royal residence, and the flower-decorated porches in the Judera (old Jewish quarter) near the Incomparable Mosque.

The Judera exudes an antiquated Moorish charm with its winding, narrow alleyways, small squares, and low, whitewashed houses.

10. The Prado and Paseo del Artes, Madrid

The Prado alone is one of the most visited tourist sites in Madrid due to the volume and caliber of its holdings. But when you factor in the Reina Sofia Public Workmanship Gallery, the Thyssen-Bornemisza Public Historical Center, and the CaixaForum—all situated along Madrid's tree-lined, mile-long lane—you might have the world's most remarkable collection of artifacts of priceless craftsmanship.

It should come as no surprise that this is the "Paseo del Arte," or Lane of Human Expression.

Expanding in 2007 to increase its presenting space, the Prado added 12 new exhibits in 2009 featuring works by Goya and other craftsmen of the late 19th century.

The Prado is home to the world's largest collection of Spanish craftsmanship, which spans an incredible spectrum from the early medieval era to the mid-20th century avant-garde growth. Among the most notable pieces from Spain's golden age are those by El Greco, Velázquez, and Goya.

Whatever the case, its wealth is not limited to Spanish art; other features are the old paintings and retablos, the creations of Flemish and Dutch masters (don't miss the dreamland of Hieronymus Bosch and the works of Brueghel and Rubens), and the Italian workmanship (Botticelli, Raphael, Correggio, Titian, and Tintoretto).

11. San Lorenzo de El Escorial

San Lorenzo de El Escorial, located roughly 45 kilometers northwest of Madrid, served as the monarchs of Spain's midyear residence. In 1563, work on a large complex that would contain a cathedral, gallery, catacomb, library, and royal residence—all significant to Philip II and his reign—began here. The outcome is an astounding assemblage of attractions centered on 16 yards, connected by 16 kilometers of hallways connecting rooms and patterns. At its heart is the assembly, centered on Herrera's 30-meter-tall retablos made of red marble and jasper that were moved toward it over the course of 17 phases.

The Panteón de los Reyes, the spectacular entombment vault of the Spanish lords, and the library, a wonderful room also enhanced with Tibaldi frescoes, are features of the religious community. These complement the Tibaldi-frescoed and domed roofs in the flats off the lower tier.

Don't miss the Whiskey Suite at the castle, which features 338 woven works of art and unusual furnishings in Charles IV's state apartments. Handcrafted private homes for Philip II are no longer in existence. The Image Exhibition below features numerous outstanding compositions by artists such as Hieronymus Bosch, Albrecht Dürer, Titian, Tintoretto, Veronese, Velázquez, and El Greco.

12. Seville Basilica and Alcázar

The Giralda tower, the Catedral de Sevilla, and the Alcázar surround a UNESCO World Heritage Site. These three exceptional and noteworthy landmarks are the main tourist attractions of Seville.

Seville's symbol, La Giralda, was formerly merely a minaret; the Extraordinary Mosque in the city was dismantled and replaced by the basilica.

With a main elevated part measuring 37 meters square and completely plated in gold, the Seville church boasts a larger interior than St. Peter's in Rome. Christopher Columbus' majestic gravesite is being held up by a group of four fantastic statues.

The Alcázar, or the house of God, was built by The Fields in 712, and after the Christian Reconquista, Pedro I restored it with lavish Mudéjar architecture (mixing Gothic and Muslim building components). With fanciful features like beautifully tiled walls and patterned ceilings, the magnificent rooms and salons are sure to delight.

Hiding among fragrant orange and lemon trees, the stunning Alcázar gardens were designed for the Round of High Positions series. Fans of the show may recognize the sources as the Water Nurseries of the Realm of Dorne.

Originally called the Judera (Jewish quarter), the Barrio de St. Nick Cruz is a neighborhood that borders the Alcázar on the east and features whitewashed homes, iron galleries, and flower-filled patios.

13. Guggenheim Gallery, Bilbao

You truly must visit this structure in person to fully comprehend it. This cluster of shapes is so vivid that they nearly look ready to take flight; no camera has ever done them justice. American draftsman Forthright Gehry employed bits of limestone and undulating titanium sheets to disrupt conventional design thinking.

His success was so great that it inspired two new terms: "architourism," which refers to an entire segment of the travel industry focused around important pieces of contemporary architecture, and "The Bilbao Impact," which refers to a city's capacity to turn its fortunes by constructing a single elite project.

The gallery covers 24,000 square meters of exhibition space, which it uses for rotating presentations of its own collections of modern craftsmanship as well as temporary exhibits.

Featured artists include Anselm Kiefer, Willem de Kooning, Mark Rothko, and Andy Warhol.

Outside of the Guggenheim Historical Center, some important social destinations in Bilbao are the Museo de Bellas Artes de Bilbao, the luxury dining scene, and the old town, or Casco Viejo. Bilbao is home to several well-known Michelin-starred restaurants, including Atelier Etxanobe, which serves inventive haute cuisine, Ola Martin Berasategui, which serves modern Spanish cuisine utilizing items from the fresh market, and Nerua, which is located in the Guggenheim Historical Center.

14. Santiago de Compostela House of God

The magnificent Santiago (St. James) house of prayer in Santiago de Compostela, built to honor the saint's relics, has been the pilgrims' final resting place since the Middle Ages. (Today's modern adventurers are lured to the medieval town of Santiago de Compostela, a popular travel destination in northern Spain's Galicia area.)

Built between 1060 and 1211, the church is a superb example of Early Romanesque architecture. Although the façade was transformed into a Rococo style in the sixteenth and eighteenth centuries, the interior has been retained in its most ideal Early Romanesque form.

You can see both of these eras at work as you make your way into the west front through one of Spain's most recognizable church exteriors. Step inside and turn to face the Pórtico de la Gloria, a portion of the old west front now obscured by a seventeenth-century veneer. This triple gateway houses one of the world's largest and most magnificent collections of Romanesque statues.

Built on top of the Messenger's burial chamber, the ornately decorated Capilla Mayor serves as the focal point of the interior design.

In the middle of the expansive unique raised platform composed of alabaster, silver, and jasper is a wooden statue dating back to the thirteenth century, exquisitely adorned with precious metals and diamonds.

Restricted staircases ascend behind the figure on one or both sides, enabling guests to kiss the shroud and complete their tour around. The missionary's bones are interred in a tomb below the distinctive stepping area in a silver casket.

15. Court Mayor, Madrid

Square Mayor, the throbbing heart of Spain's dynamic capital city, has had a significant influence on Madrid's everyday life ever since Philip II divided the planning duties with his chief planner, Juan de Herrera, in the sixteenth century.

The Plaza Mayor has served as a venue for public entertainment such as bullfights and chivalric contests, as well as ceremonial events like the canonization of saints, the declaration of another ruler, and the eating of blasphemers for a long time. Today, it is one of Madrid's most popular social destinations.

The restaurants that spill out onto the square's main stone pavement and those hidden behind its arcades make up Madrid's lounge. These places are popular with locals and tourists alike for socializing.

One of the best areas to stay is in the vicinity of Plaza Mayor, which acts as the center of public life in Madrid. Just a short drive from the Square Mayor, the four-star Catalonia Las Cortes has family-friendly visiting rooms and accommodations right next to the

Prado Exhibition Hall, which is perfect for artists.

16. Court de Espaa and Parque de Mara Luisa, Seville

Encircled by hallways, the magnificent semi-round Square of Spain was built for the 1929 Ibero-American Composition in remembrance of the many Spanish districts.

The large pool, divided by spans, is overlooked in favor of beautiful boards adorned with vibrant ornamental tiles representing the various provinces of Spain. It's a popular spot for strolls or for navigating a rental boat beneath the extensions and around the pool.

Gathering at the Court de Espana is the vast Parque de Maria Luisa, a half-mile ribbon of nurseries, yards, and secret promenades stretching near the waterway that obliquely focuses Seville. On the other hand, you can rent a pedal vehicle or ride in a pony-drawn carriage. On Sundays, the recreation area is packed with families.

The greatest way to take in the goliath trees, blossom beds, lakes, gazebos, and man-made rock mountain with a waterfall is to stroll around the recreation area and into the surrounding gardens. A little but rich prehistoric historical center with Visigoth jeweled peevish and antique gold craftsmanship may be found at the far end of the leisure area.

17. Ciudad de las Artes y las Ciencias, Valencia

Valencia was left with a wide, level riverbank that was separated by bridges when the river that had swallowed the city reversed its course. Admirers of modern engineering have been lured to the impressive collection of ideas created by the gifted Spanish architect Santiago Calatrava on this flawless line.

But the structures and the galleries and the beautiful settings and the aquarium (which was designed by Félix Candela; Calatrava's main building is not one of them) combine to create a string of tourist attractions that catapult Spain into the global spotlight.

Constructed in the form of a water lily, L'Oceanogràfic is the biggest oceanographic aquarium in Europe, with structures that depict a range of marine habitats, from the tropics to the poles.

Convenience: The Greatest Valencia Hotels and Neighborhoods

18. Gran Canaria's beaches

Gran Canaria is the most famous of the Canary Islands because of its beautiful sand beaches, which occupy most of the island's southern shore. Families love Playa de Las Canteras in the capital city of Las Palmas because of its serene waters shielded by a unique volcanic stone sea wall.

The biggest and busiest beach in Maspalomas is called Playa del Inglés, and it has lots of shops, restaurants, cafes, playgrounds, and other amenities. Situated on one side of the archipelago is a typical pond, enclosed by a large protected area of massive sand hills.

These can reach heights of up to 12 meters and are produced by the breeze and the water. They never stop moving. To finish the desert trick, you can ride a camel across this otherwise ordinary yet dilapidated location.

Given that this area typically has warm water, it should come as no surprise that surfers frequent this area.

There's a submerged park at Arinaga, diving schools near Playa del Inglés, and a few additional spots along the shore. On the other hand, a trip in a glass-lined boat lets you observe the fish and other aquatic life. On the south beach, windsurfing and cruising are also quite popular activities.

19. La Rambla, Barcelona

Strolling down La Rambla on a summer's evening could give you the sense that everyone in Barcelona is there. Without a doubt, it's the greatest place to go after work on a weeknight or a mid-summer evening. This tree-lined roadway cuts a somewhat crooked green line through the heart of the city, heading northwest from the Columbus Dedication near the harbor.

Plane trees line the part leading to the Plaça de Catalunya, and narrow streets run on either side of the large common area.

In addition to its flower and bird markets, La Rambla is home to a plethora of book and paper businesses, eateries, and bistros with outdoor seating.

Live sculptures, road artists, entertainers on the spur of the moment, and asphalt artisans all contribute to the vibrant atmosphere.

One of the features of La Rambla is the Mercat de la Boqueria (91 Rambla), a historic covered market center that sells fresh vegetables, meat, fish, bread, cheese, and other specialty delicacies. To obtain the ingredients for their homemade feasts, locals travel here. The opportunity to taste local cuisine at the market's tapas bars will be much appreciated by visitors.

20. El Teide, Tenerife

At Spain's highest point is an ancient, but boiling, fountain of liquid magma, one of Europe's greatest regular miracles. The Pico del Teide and the large volcanic depression known as the Caldera de las Caadas comprise the Parque Nacional del Teide, which is located in the center of the island of Tenerife. When UNESCO announced its designation of the leisure area in 2007, it cited "its value in affording proof of the land processes that enable the development of maritime islands" in addition to its regular quality.

There are several of ways to find out more information on El Teide. You may drive or walk the whole 12-mile-wide caldera's bottom, which is encircled by a desolate moonscape of patterned rock formations that seem to be colliding with the earth's core.

Although it is possible to climb El Teide's cone, a shorter and easier route to get near the top is to take an eight-minute trolley trip. The sun can be seen lighting up the entire archipelago of the Canary Islands, which are the closest continent to North Africa.

21. Toledo's Old City

Perhaps his most famous painting, "The City," depicts the blending of Moorish, Gothic, and Renaissance architectural styles. Toledo, a middle-aged city with a distinctive profile, is approached from below. The city is located high on a rocky slope and is encircled on three sides by the deep Tagus Waterway gap.

The various churches, religious institutions, and hospices show the engineering of the Christian era, but the town's layout, with its occasional tiny alleys and several secret back passageways, reflects its Moorish past.

Because of this, the Casco Histórico (Old Town) has been acknowledged by UNESCO as a component of the social legacy of humanity and functions as a kind of outdoor gallery defining Spain's historical setting.

Thanks to its fully renovated interior, Toledo's magnificent Gothic Cathedral is one of the most popular tourist sights in the city. The two gathering places in the barometrically constructed medieval Judera (Jewish neighborhood) are richly decorated in a Moorish style. Make sure to see the El Greco artwork in the congregation of Santo Tomé in the Judera.

Summarizing: Spain features a number of well-known architectural structures. Spain's architecture is a fascinating fusion of early Moorish, European, and bizarre modernist styles. The many foreign influences on Spain's national culture also had a significant impact on the country's art and architecture. From the old Roman reflection to the most modern and contemporary style, Spain takes pride in all of its best buildings.

Chapter 3: Itineraries

Why you need itinerary

Efficient Planning & Organization:

- **Maximize Time**: An itinerary assists you in making the most of your trip by ranking the sights, events, and activities according to your interests, preferences, and time constraints. It guarantees that you efficiently cover the must-see locations, monuments, and sites in Spain, saving you time when it comes to planning and making decisions.

2. Budget Management:

- **Cost Estimation**: You may successfully budget and manage resources based on goals, preferences, and financial limits by planning your schedule and anticipating costs associated with lodging, transportation, attractions, meals, and activities.
- **Value Optimization**: An itinerary helps you identify cost-effective options, promotions, discounts, and package deals for accommodations, transportation, attractions, and experiences in Spain, maximizing value and minimizing unnecessary expenses or overspending.

3. Cultural & Regional Exploration:

- **Diverse Experiences**: A carefully thought-out schedule is required to fully experience Spain's dynamic cities, coastal areas, mountains, islands, and cultural sites due to the country's different regions, cultures, landscapes, and traditions. Through a variety of locations and experiences, it allows you to fully immerse yourself in Spain's rich

heritage, gastronomic delights, cultural legacy, and sense of community.
- **Seasonal Considerations**: By arranging your itinerary to coincide with local customs, traditions, celebrations, and seasonal activities that suit your interests and tastes, you can make the most of your trip to Spain by tailoring it to particular seasons, festivals, events, and area attractions.

4. Logistics & Transportation:

- **Travel Coordination**: By planning modes of transportation (such as buses, trains, flights, and rental cars) between locations, maximizing routes, and guaranteeing punctual arrivals and departures during your trip in Spain, an itinerary makes travel planning easier.
- **Accessibility & Convenience**: Planning your itinerary allows you to assess transportation options, accessibility, connectivity, and logistics (e.g., luggage storage, transfers, connections) for navigating Spain's diverse regions, attractions, and destinations comfortably, safely, and efficiently.

5. Flexibility & Adaptability:

- **Structured Framework**: An itinerary gives you a general idea of where to go in Spain, but you also need to be able to adjust and be flexible in response to unforeseen events, changes in plans, the weather, advice from locals, and personal preferences. Including downtime, leisure pursuits, unwinding, and impromptu encounters improves your trip and makes discovering Spain's fascinating towns, villages, and landscapes even more enjoyable.

6. Safety & Security:

- **Preparedness**: An itinerary promotes safety and security by

researching destinations, assessing potential risks, understanding local laws, regulations, and cultural norms, and preparing adequately for emergencies, health concerns, and unexpected situations while traveling in Spain.
- **Peace of Mind**: Having a well-planned itinerary provides peace of mind, confidence, and reassurance during your Spain trip, knowing you've prepared, organized, and considered essential factors, considerations, and contingencies to ensure a memorable, enjoyable, and fulfilling travel experience.

one-week itinerary

Day 1: Arrival in Madrid

- **Morning**:
    - Arrive in Madrid and check into your hotel.
    - Rest and refresh after your journey.
- **Afternoon**:
    - Explore the historic center of Madrid, starting with Puerta del Sol, Plaza Mayor, and Mercado San Miguel.
    - Visit the Royal Palace of Madrid and Almudena Cathedral.
- **Evening**:
    - Enjoy dinner at a local restaurant specializing in traditional Spanish cuisine.
    - Wander through the lively streets of Madrid and experience the city's vibrant nightlife.

Day 2: Madrid - Art & Culture

- **Morning**:
    - Visit the Prado Museum, home to masterpieces by Goya, Velázquez, and El Greco.
- **Afternoon**:
    - Explore the Thyssen-Bornemisza Museum and Reina

- Sofia Museum.
- Relax in Retiro Park, Madrid's green oasis, and enjoy a leisurely stroll or boat ride on the lake.
- **Evening**:
  - Dine in the trendy neighborhoods of Chueca or Malasaña.
  - Experience a flamenco show or live music performance in Madrid's cultural venues.

Day 3: Madrid to Barcelona

- **Morning**:
  - Travel to Barcelona via high-speed train or flight.
  - Check into your hotel in Barcelona.
- **Afternoon**:
  - Explore La Rambla, Barcelona's bustling pedestrian boulevard.
  - Visit the Gothic Quarter, including Barcelona Cathedral and Plaça del Rei.
- **Evening**:
  - Enjoy dinner at a seafood restaurant in Barceloneta.
  - Experience Barcelona's nightlife in El Raval or El Born neighborhoods.

Day 4: Barcelona - Gaudí's Masterpieces

- **Morning**:
  - Visit La Sagrada Familia, Gaudí's iconic basilica.
- **Afternoon**:
  - Explore Park Güell, admiring Gaudí's architectural designs and panoramic views of Barcelona.
  - Visit Casa Batlló and Casa Milà along Passeig de Gràcia.
- **Evening**:
  - Dine in Eixample district, known for its gastronomic diversity.
  - Experience a rooftop bar or terrace offering stunning

views of Barcelona's skyline.

Day 5: Barcelona - Montjuïc & Beaches

- **Morning**:
  - Explore Montjuïc Hill, including Montjuïc Castle, Magic Fountain, and National Art Museum of Catalonia.
- **Afternoon**:
  - Relax and unwind at Barceloneta Beach, enjoying the Mediterranean sun, sea, and sand.
  - Explore Port Vell and Maremagnum, a vibrant waterfront area with shopping, dining, and entertainment options.
- **Evening**:
  - Enjoy a seafood dinner overlooking the Mediterranean Sea.
  - Stroll along the beach promenade, experiencing Barcelona's coastal charm and nightlife.

Day 6: Day Trip - Montserrat or Girona

- **Option 1: Montserrat**:
  - Embark on a day trip to Montserrat, exploring the Benedictine monastery, stunning landscapes, and hiking trails.
  - Experience the Montserrat Boys' Choir and enjoy panoramic views of Catalonia.
- **Option 2: Girona**:
  - Travel to Girona and explore its historic Old Town, Jewish Quarter, and iconic landmarks, including Girona Cathedral and Arab Baths.
  - Enjoy local cuisine, culture, and scenic beauty of Girona's picturesque landscapes.

Day 7: Departure or Leisure

- **Morning**:
  - Depending on your departure time, explore any remaining sights, neighborhoods, or experiences in Madrid or Barcelona.
- **Afternoon**:
  - Depart from Spain or spend leisure time exploring local markets, shopping districts, or enjoying a relaxing day in one of the cities.
- **Evening**:
  - Departure from Barcelona or continue your journey in Spain, exploring additional regions, cities, or attractions based on your interests and travel plans.

two-week itinerary

Day 1-3: Madrid - Capital City Exploration

- **Day 1**:
  - **Accommodation**: Stay centrally located near Puerta del Sol or Plaza Mayor for easy access to Madrid's attractions, dining, and nightlife.
  - **Food & Drink**: Experience traditional Spanish cuisine, including tapas, paella, churros, and local wines.
  - **Shopping**: Explore Gran Vía, Calle Preciados, and local markets for souvenirs, fashion, crafts, and gourmet products.
- **Day 2**:
  - **Museums**: Reserve tickets in advance for the Prado Museum, Reina Sofia Museum, and Thyssen-Bornemisza Museum to explore art collections, exhibitions, and cultural events.
  - **Parks & Gardens**: Enjoy a leisurely afternoon in El Retiro Park, exploring gardens, sculptures, boating lake, and outdoor performances.

- **Evening Entertainment**: Attend a flamenco show, theater performance, or concert in Madrid's cultural venues, theaters, and entertainment districts.
- **Day 3**:
    - **Day Trip**: Embark on a day trip to Toledo, Segovia, or Ávila to explore UNESCO World Heritage sites, historical landmarks, and cultural heritage of Castile and Leon region.

Day 4-6: Seville - Andalusian Charm & Heritage

- **Day 4**:
    - **Accommodation**: Stay in Seville's historic center or Santa Cruz neighborhood to immerse yourself in Andalusian architecture, culture, and traditions.
    - **Culinary Experiences**: Explore local markets, tapas bars, and restaurants to savor Sevillian cuisine, including gazpacho, fried fish, jamón ibérico, and traditional desserts.
- **Day 5**:
    - **Landmarks**: Visit Seville Cathedral, climb the Giralda Tower, explore Real Alcázar, and wander through Barrio Santa Cruz, the former Jewish quarter.
    - **Flamenco**: Attend a flamenco performance in a local tablao or cultural venue, experiencing the passion, music, and dance of Andalusia.
- **Day 6**:
    - **Day Trip**: Explore Jerez de la Frontera, Cádiz, or Ronda, experiencing sherry wine tasting, coastal landscapes, ancient ruins, and white-washed villages of Andalusia.

Day 7-9: Granada - Moorish Legacy & Sierra Nevada

- **Day 7**:
    - **Accommodation**: Stay near the Alhambra Palace or Albayzín neighborhood to explore Granada's Moorish

heritage, cultural sites, and Sierra Nevada mountains.
- **Alhambra**: Reserve tickets in advance for the Alhambra Palace, Generalife Gardens, and Nasrid Palaces to explore architectural marvels, gardens, and panoramic views of Granada.
- **Day 8**:
  - **Sierra Nevada**: Embark on a day trip to Sierra Nevada National Park, hiking, skiing, or exploring natural landscapes, flora, fauna, and outdoor activities in the mountains.
  - **Cuisine**: Experience Granada's culinary scene, including tapas bars, local markets, and Andalusian specialties, such as Sacromonte omelette, piononos, and Moroccan-inspired dishes.
- **Day 9**:
  - **Albaicín & Sacromonte**: Explore Granada's historic neighborhoods, including Albaicín's Moorish architecture, viewpoints, and narrow streets, and Sacromonte's caves, flamenco culture, and panoramic views.

Day 10-12: Valencia - Mediterranean Coast & Modernist Architecture

- **Day 10**:
  - **Accommodation**: Stay near Valencia's City of Arts and Sciences, beaches, and cultural attractions, exploring the modernist architecture, gastronomy, and coastal charm.
  - **City of Arts and Sciences**: Visit modernist landmarks, including L'Hemisfèric, Science Museum, Oceanogràfic, and Palau de les Arts Reina Sofía.
- **Day 11**:
  - **Turia Gardens**: Explore Turia Gardens, a green oasis, sports, leisure activities, and cultural events along the former riverbed, connecting Valencia's landmarks, neighborhoods, and attractions.

- **Culinary Delights**: Experience Valencia's gastronomy, including paella, horchata, tapas, and local wines, exploring markets, restaurants, and traditional eateries.
- Day 12:
  - **Beaches & Coastal Attractions**: Relax and unwind at Valencia's beaches, marinas, and waterfront areas, enjoying water sports, sunbathing, and seaside dining options along the Mediterranean coast.

Day 13-14: Barcelona - Modernist Marvels & Mediterranean Magic

- Day 13:
  - **Accommodation**: Stay in Barcelona's Eixample district, Gothic Quarter, or waterfront area, exploring Gaudí's masterpieces, cultural landmarks, and vibrant neighborhoods.
  - **Gaudí's Architecture**: Visit La Sagrada Familia, Park Güell, Casa Batlló, and Casa Milà, experiencing Gaudí's architectural designs, innovations, and iconic landmarks.
- Day 14:
  - **Barcelona Highlights**: Explore additional sights, neighborhoods, and experiences in Barcelona, such as Montjuïc Hill, Barceloneta Beach, Gothic Quarter, and Passeig de Gràcia.
  - **Farewell Dinner**: Enjoy a farewell dinner, reflecting on your Spain journey, experiences, memories, and highlights in Barcelona or Madrid before departing.

Weekend Itinerary: Barcelona, Catalonia

Day 1: Friday - Arrival & Gothic Quarter Exploration

- **Morning**:
  - Arrive in Barcelona and check into your hotel, ideally

    located in the Gothic Quarter or Eixample district.
  - Enjoy a light breakfast at a local café or bakery, sampling Catalan pastries and coffee.
- **Afternoon**:
  - Explore the Gothic Quarter, wandering through narrow streets, medieval architecture, and historical landmarks.
  - Visit Barcelona Cathedral, Plaça del Rei, and Roman ruins at the Museu d'Història de Barcelona (MUHBA).
- **Evening**:
  - Dine at a traditional tapas bar in El Born or Barri Gòtic, sampling local specialties, such as patatas bravas, jamón ibérico, and Catalan wines.
  - Experience Barcelona's nightlife with a cocktail at a rooftop bar, live music venue, or beachfront club.

Day 2: Saturday - Modernist Marvels & La Rambla

- **Morning**:
  - Breakfast at a local café or brunch spot, enjoying Catalan flavors, fresh ingredients, and Mediterranean cuisine.
  - Explore Passeig de Gràcia, admiring Gaudí's architectural masterpieces, including Casa Batlló and Casa Milà.
- **Afternoon**:
  - Visit La Sagrada Familia, experiencing Gaudí's unfinished basilica, architectural innovations, and spiritual atmosphere.
  - Stroll along La Rambla, Barcelona's iconic boulevard, exploring street performers, markets, and historic landmarks, such as the Liceu Opera House and Plaça de Catalunya.
- **Evening**:
  - Dine at a seafood restaurant in Barceloneta, enjoying Mediterranean dishes, fresh catches, and seaside views.
  - Experience Barcelona's nightlife, dining, entertainment, and cultural events in El Raval, El Born, or Port Vell

districts.

Day 3: Sunday - Montjuïc Hill & Beach Relaxation

- **Morning**:
    - Breakfast at your hotel or a nearby café, enjoying Catalan specialties, coffee, and pastries before exploring Montjuïc Hill.
    - Take a cable car or funicular to Montjuïc, exploring cultural attractions, such as Montjuïc Castle, Magic Fountain, and National Art Museum of Catalonia (MNAC).
- **Afternoon**:
    - Relax and unwind at Barceloneta Beach, enjoying sunbathing, swimming, water sports, and seaside dining options along the Mediterranean coast.
    - Explore Port Vell, Maremagnum, or La Barceloneta, experiencing waterfront attractions, shopping, dining, and leisure activities.
- **Evening**:
    - Enjoy a farewell dinner in a waterfront restaurant, reflecting on your weekend in Barcelona, experiences, and memories.
    - Experience Barcelona's vibrant nightlife, cultural events, or leisurely evening stroll along the beach promenade.

Departure:

- Depending on your departure time, explore local markets, shops, or neighborhoods, enjoying a final taste of Barcelona before departing.
- Depart from Barcelona, reflecting on your weekend itinerary, experiences, and memories in Catalonia's vibrant capital city.

Chapter 4:
Best Restaurants and Cuisine

The development of Spanish cuisine has been influenced by numerous civilizations, including the Romans, Moors, Jews, and Christians, as well as centuries of historical events and cultural interactions. Olive oil, grapes, and wine were brought by Phoenician traders, and farming, livestock, and culinary customs were impacted by Roman invasions. The introduction of rice, spices, nuts, and fruits during the Moorish era revolutionized Spanish cuisine by introducing novel cooking methods, tastes, and ingredients. Spanish cuisine, pastries, and sweets were influenced by Jewish communities' dietary regulations, preservation techniques, and culinary customs.

Culinary Techniques & Traditions:

- **Preservation**: The preservation of meats, fish, vegetables, and fruits using techniques like pickling, smoking, curing, and drying enhances their flavors, textures, and shelf life and is highly valued in Spanish cuisine.
- **Frying**: Spanish gastronomy makes extensive use of frying methods, such as deep-frying, pan-frying, and shallow-frying, which result in crispy, savory meals like churros, croquettes, and fried seafood.
- **Grilling & Roasting**: Spain's culinary traditions emphasize grilling, roasting, and barbecuing techniques, showcasing meats, seafood, vegetables, and fruits' natural flavors, aromas, and textures in traditional dishes and regional specialties.

Regional Variations & Specialties:

- **Northern Spain**: Asturias, Cantabria, and the Basque Country feature seafood dishes, bean stews, mountain

cuisine, cider, and pintxos (Basque tapas).
- **Central Spain**: Castilla-La Mancha, Castilla y León, and Madrid showcase hearty stews, roast meats, Manchego cheese, sausages, and traditional desserts.
- **Eastern Spain**: Catalonia, Valencia, and the Balearic Islands emphasize rice dishes, seafood paellas, fideuà, tapas, and regional wines.
- **Southern Spain**: Andalusia, Extremadura, and Murcia highlight gazpacho, salmorejo, fried fish, Moorish-influenced dishes, sherry wines, and culinary traditions.

Key Ingredients & Staples:

- **Olive Oil**: High-quality olive oil is produced by Spain's many olive orchards and is vital for seasoning, frying, dressing, and cooking food. It also has health benefits.
- **Saffron**: Spanish saffron, sometimes referred to as "red gold," adds a distinct flavor, perfume, and vivid color to rice dishes, stews, soups, sauces, and desserts.
- **Paprika**: Spanish paprika (pimentón) varieties, including sweet, bittersweet, and hot, add smoky, spicy, and flavorful nuances to dishes, enhancing meats, stews, seafood, and vegetables.

Desserts, Pastries & Sweets:

Almonds, honey, chocolate, citrus fruits, and other traditional ingredients are cherished in Spanish desserts, pastries, and sweets, as well as in traditional recipes, regional specialties, and joyful events. Traditional Spanish sweets such as flan, churros, marzipan, polvorones, turrón, and mantecados highlight the nation's sweet traditions, gastronomic heritage, and celebratory occasions.

To taste the rich and varied flavors of Spanish cuisine, travelers should try these 15 regional specialties from different parts of Spain:

1. Paella Valenciana (Valencia)

Valencia's signature rice dish, paella, is a representation of Spain's rich culinary legacy and regional specialties. It is cooked with saffron-infused rice and contains local vegetables, chicken, rabbit, and beans.

2. Gazpacho (Andalusia)

Gazpacho, a cool soup made with tomatoes, peppers, cucumbers, onions, garlic, vinegar, olive oil, and bread, showcases the tastes, freshness, and culinary traditions of Andalusia.

3. Cocido Madrileño (Madrid)

A hearty chickpea stew featuring meats, sausages, vegetables, and spices, cocido madrileño emphasizes Madrid's comfort food, seasonal ingredients, and regional flavors.

4. Tapas (Throughout Spain)

Small plates, appetizers, or snacks showcasing Spain's diverse ingredients, flavors, and culinary traditions, tapas highlight regional specialties, innovative dishes, and social dining experiences.

5. Pintxos (Basque Country)

Basque-style tapas featuring skewered bites, pintxos showcase local ingredients, innovative flavors, and culinary creativity in San Sebastián's bars, taverns, and eateries.

6. Salmorejo (Andalusia)

A creamy cold soup made from tomatoes, bread, olive oil, garlic, and vinegar, salmorejo highlights Cordoba's culinary traditions, flavors, and regional specialties.

7. Fabada Asturiana (Asturias)

A hearty bean stew featuring Asturian white beans, chorizo, morcilla, pork belly, and saffron, fabada asturiana emphasizes northern Spain's mountain cuisine, flavors, and hearty dishes.

8. Cava (Catalonia)

A sparkling wine produced in Catalonia's Penedès region, cava showcases Spain's wine-making traditions, grape varieties, and festive celebrations.

9. Jamón Ibérico (Throughout Spain)

Cured ham from Iberian pigs, jamón ibérico highlights Spain's preservation methods, quality ingredients, and culinary traditions in traditional bars, restaurants, and markets.

10. Turron (Throughout Spain)

A traditional nougat dessert made from almonds, honey, sugar, and egg whites, turron highlights Spain's festive sweets, regional variations, and cultural celebrations.

11. Txakoli (Basque Country)

A crisp, dry white wine produced in the Basque Country's coastal vineyards, txakoli showcases northern Spain's wine regions, grape varieties, and gastronomic traditions.

12. Pulpo a la Gallega (Galicia)

Galician-style octopus featuring boiled octopus, paprika, olive oil, and potatoes, pulpo a la gallega highlights Galicia's coastal cuisine, seafood dishes, and traditional flavors.

13. Crema Catalana (Catalonia)

A creamy custard dessert featuring caramelized sugar, cinnamon, and citrus zest, crema catalana showcases Catalonia's sweet traditions, festive celebrations, and regional specialties.

14. Fideuà (Valencia)

A noodle paella featuring short noodles, seafood, fish, tomatoes, garlic, paprika, and saffron, fideuà highlights Valencia's culinary traditions, coastal flavors, and regional specialties.

15. Churros con Chocolate (Throughout Spain)

Deep-fried dough pastry served with thick hot chocolate for dipping, churros con chocolate highlight Spain's sweet breakfasts, traditional treats, and culinary indulgences.

Restaurants

Tapas Bars & Taverns:

- **El Xampanyet (Barcelona, Catalonia):**
  - *Description*: A historic tapas bar in Barcelona's El Born neighborhood, known for its traditional Catalan tapas, house-made cava, and lively atmosphere.
- **Cervecería Catalana (Barcelona, Catalonia):**
  - *Description*: A bustling tapas bar in the Eixample district, offering a wide selection of tapas, including patatas bravas, grilled octopus, and Iberian ham.
- **El Rinconcillo (Seville, Andalusia):**
  - *Description*: Established in 1670, El Rinconcillo is one of Seville's oldest tapas bars, known for its traditional Andalusian tapas, charming decor, and historic ambiance.
- **Casa Labra (Madrid):**
  - *Description*: A historic tavern in Madrid, Casa Labra is famous for its bacalao (salted cod) croquettes and

vermouth, providing a taste of traditional Madrid tapas.
- **La Cuchara de San Telmo (San Sebastián, Basque Country):**
  - *Description*: Located in the heart of San Sebastián's Old Town, this pintxos bar is renowned for its creative and flavorful Basque-style small bites, such as grilled octopus and foie gras.

2. **Restaurants & Gastronomic Establishments:**

- **El Celler de Can Roca (Girona, Catalonia):**
  - *Description*: A three-Michelin-starred restaurant, El Celler de Can Roca is known for its avant-garde Catalan cuisine, innovative tasting menus, and exceptional dining experience.
- **DiverXO (Madrid):**
  - *Description*: A Michelin-starred restaurant in Madrid, DiverXO offers a fusion of Spanish and Asian flavors, with a dynamic menu crafted by Chef David Muñoz.
- **Tickets Bar (Barcelona, Catalonia):**
  - *Description*: Co-owned by the Adrià brothers, Tickets Bar is a culinary adventure featuring creative tapas, molecular gastronomy, and playful presentations.
- **Azurmendi (Larrabetzu, Basque Country):**
  - *Description*: A three-Michelin-starred restaurant in the Basque Country, Azurmendi is known for its sustainable practices, modern Basque cuisine, and innovative tasting menus.
- **Botín (Madrid):**
  - *Description*: Established in 1725, Botín is recognized by the Guinness World Records as the world's oldest restaurant. Known for its classic Spanish dishes, it's a cultural and culinary landmark in Madrid.

3. **Chiringuitos & Beach Bars:**

   - **Chiringuito Pez Vela (Barcelona, Catalonia):**
     - *Description*: Located on Barceloneta Beach, Chiringuito Pez Vela offers seafood paellas, grilled fish, and cocktails with stunning views of the Mediterranean Sea.
   - **El Tintero (Malaga, Andalusia):**
     - *Description*: A unique seafood chiringuito in Malaga where waiters parade with trays of fresh catches, and diners signal for their desired dishes.
   - **Nassau Beach Club (Ibiza, Balearic Islands):**
     - *Description*: A chic beach club in Ibiza, Nassau Beach Club offers Mediterranean cuisine, cocktails, and a vibrant atmosphere right on the beach.
   - **Chiringuito Toni (Valencia):**
     - *Description*: A popular beachside spot in Valencia, Chiringuito Toni serves paellas, grilled seafood, and refreshing drinks, creating a relaxed and casual beach experience.
   - **Sa Punta (Ibiza, Balearic Islands):**
     - *Description*: Located in Talamanca Bay, Sa Punta offers a stylish beachfront setting with a diverse menu featuring fresh seafood, sushi, and Mediterranean dishes.

4. **Markets & Food Halls:**

   - **Mercado de San Miguel (Madrid):**
     - *Description*: A historic market in Madrid's city center, Mercado de San Miguel features gourmet stalls offering a variety of tapas, fresh produce, and artisanal products.
   - **La Boqueria (Barcelona, Catalonia):**
     - *Description*: One of Europe's most famous markets, La Boqueria in Barcelona is a bustling marketplace with vibrant stalls selling fresh fruits, meats, seafood, and tapas.
   - **Mercado Central (Valencia):**

- *Description*: Valencia's Mercado Central is a lively food market with colorful stalls selling fresh produce, meats, cheeses, and local specialties like horchata.
- **Mercado de Triana (Seville, Andalusia):**
  - *Description*: Located in the Triana neighborhood, this traditional market offers a wide array of fresh products, local wines, and Andalusian specialties.
- **Mercat de Santa Caterina (Barcelona, Catalonia):**
  - *Description*: Known for its unique undulating roof, Mercat de Santa Caterina in Barcelona features stalls offering fresh seafood, meats, cheeses, and Catalan products.

5. Bodegas & Wine Bars (Continued):

- **Bodegas Ysios (La Rioja):**
  - *Description*: Located in the heart of La Rioja's wine country, Bodegas Ysios is renowned for its avant-garde architecture, offering guided tours, wine tastings, and breathtaking views of the vineyards and Sierra de Cantabria mountains.
- **Bodegas López de Heredia Viña Tondonia (La Rioja):**
  - *Description*: A historic winery founded in 1877, López de Heredia is famous for its traditional winemaking techniques, aged Riojas, and guided tours of its underground cellars, oak barrels, and vineyards.
- **Bodega Caelum (Barcelona, Catalonia):**
  - *Description*: Located in Barcelona's Gothic Quarter, Bodega Caelum offers a unique wine and artisanal shop specializing in Catalan wines, local products, tastings, and gourmet experiences.
- **Bodegas Muga (La Rioja):**
  - *Description*: A family-owned winery in Haro, Bodegas Muga offers guided tours, wine tastings, and a glimpse into its traditional winemaking process, including barrel aging, fermentation, and bottling.

- **Vinoteca Moratín (Madrid):**
  - *Description*: A cozy wine bar in Madrid's literary quarter, Vinoteca Moratín offers a curated selection of Spanish wines, tapas, charcuterie, and gourmet products, providing a taste of Spain's diverse wine regions and varietals.

6. Sidrerías & Cider Houses:

- **Sidrería Petritegi (Asturias):**
  - *Description*: Located near San Sebastián, Sidrería Petritegi offers a traditional Asturian cider house experience with cider tastings, grilled meats, chorizo, and communal dining in a rustic and authentic setting.
- **Sidrería El Molín de la Pedrera (Gijón, Asturias):**
  - *Description*: A charming cider house in Gijón, El Molín de la Pedrera offers traditional Asturian cuisine, cider pouring, grilled fish, and regional dishes in a picturesque countryside setting.
- **Sagardoetxea (Basque Country):**
  - *Description*: Located in Astigarraga, Sagardoetxea is a cider museum and tasting center showcasing Basque cider culture, traditions, and gastronomy through guided tours, tastings, and exhibitions.
- **Zelaia Sagardotegia (San Sebastián, Basque Country):**
  - *Description*: A traditional Basque cider house in San Sebastián, Zelaia Sagardotegia offers cider tastings, grilled steaks, chorizo, and authentic Basque dishes in a lively and festive atmosphere.
- **Sidrería Astarbe (Asturias):**
  - *Description*: Nestled in the Asturian countryside, Sidrería Astarbe offers a traditional cider house experience with cider pouring, grilled meats, chorizo, and communal dining in a rustic and authentic setting.

7. Cafés & Bakeries:

- **Café de Oriente (Madrid):**
  - *Description*: Situated opposite the Royal Palace in Madrid, Café de Oriente offers a historic setting, elegant décor, and outdoor terrace dining. Visitors can enjoy coffee, pastries, Spanish desserts, and light meals with stunning views of the Royal Palace and Opera House.
- **Granja Dulcinea (Barcelona, Catalonia):**
  - *Description*: A traditional chocolatería and pastry shop in Barcelona, Granja Dulcinea is renowned for its thick hot chocolate, churros, pastries, and classic Catalan sweets in a charming and nostalgic atmosphere.
- **Casa Mira (Madrid):**
  - *Description*: Founded in 1855, Casa Mira is a historic confectionery shop in Madrid, offering traditional Spanish sweets, marzipan, turrón, candies, and artisanal products, showcasing Spain's sweet traditions and gourmet delights.
- **Forn Mistral (Barcelona, Catalonia):**
  - *Description*: A traditional bakery in Barcelona's Eixample district, Forn Mistral offers a variety of bread, pastries, empanadas, sandwiches, and Catalan specialties, providing a taste of authentic Catalan baked goods and flavors.
- **La Colmena (Alicante, Valencia):**
  - *Description*: A historic pastry shop in Alicante, La Colmena is famous for its almond-based sweets, turrones, marzipan, chocolates, and local pastries, celebrating Valencia's sweet traditions and gastronomic heritage.

8. Gastro Markets & Food Halls:

- **Mercado de San Antón (Madrid):**
  - *Description*: Located in Madrid's Chueca neighborhood,

Mercado de San Antón is a modern market featuring gourmet stalls, tapas bars, restaurants, and a rooftop terrace offering fresh produce, international cuisines, and culinary experiences.

- **Mercado de la Ribera (Bilbao, Basque Country):**
    - *Description*: One of Europe's largest covered markets, Mercado de la Ribera in Bilbao offers a wide variety of stalls selling fresh produce, seafood, meats, pintxos bars, and Basque specialties in a bustling and vibrant atmosphere.
- **Mercado de Santa Catalina (Barcelona, Catalonia):**
    - *Description*: Located near Barcelona's Gothic Quarter, Mercado de Santa Catalina offers a local market experience with fresh produce, seafood, meats, tapas bars, restaurants, and Catalan specialties, providing visitors with a taste of authentic Barcelona flavors and ingredients.
- **Mercado de Atarazanas (Malaga, Andalusia):**
    - *Description*: A historic market in Malaga, Mercado de Atarazanas offers a vibrant atmosphere with colorful stalls selling fresh seafood, fruits, vegetables, meats, tapas bars, and local products, showcasing Andalusian flavors, ingredients, and gastronomic traditions.
- **Mercado Central (Zaragoza, Aragon):**
    - *Description*: Zaragoza's Mercado Central is a bustling food market with diverse stalls offering fresh produce, meats, seafood, cheeses, wines, tapas bars, and regional Aragonese specialties, providing visitors with a culinary journey through Spain's diverse regions, flavors, and traditions.

Chapter 5: Accommodations in Spain

Numerous lodging options are available in Spain to accommodate a range of travel styles, budgets, and tastes. Below is a summary of well-liked lodging choices for travelers visiting Spain:

1. Hotels & Resorts:

- **Luxury Hotels:**
    1. **Hotel Arts Barcelona (Barcelona, Catalonia)**: Overlooking the Mediterranean Sea, featuring luxurious rooms, a spa, two outdoor pools, and contemporary art throughout the hotel.
    2. **Gran Meliá Palacio de los Duques (Madrid)**: Situated in a historic palace, offering elegant accommodations, a wellness center, garden, and exclusive dining experiences.
    3. **Marbella Club Hotel (Marbella, Andalusia)**: A beachfront resort with luxurious rooms, a spa, golf course, beach club, and multiple dining options.
    4. **Hotel Alfonso XIII (Seville, Andalusia)**: A landmark hotel with Moorish architecture, offering luxury rooms, a swimming pool, gardens, and Andalusian cuisine.
    5. **W Barcelona (Barcelona, Catalonia)**: Iconic sail-shaped hotel with modern design, offering sea views, a rooftop bar, infinity pool, and beach access.
- **Boutique Hotels:**
    1. **Mercer Hotel Barcelona (Barcelona, Catalonia)**: Located in El Born district, offering personalized services, a rooftop terrace, spa, and historical charm.
    2. **Cotton House Hotel (Barcelona, Catalonia)**: Housed in a 19th-century building, featuring stylish interiors, a rooftop pool, library, and sophisticated ambiance.
    3. **Hotel Cort (Palma de Mallorca, Balearic Islands)**:

Boutique hotel in Old Town Palma, offering chic rooms, a rooftop terrace, and Mediterranean charm.
4. **URSO Hotel & Spa (Madrid)**: Boutique hotel in a restored palace, featuring a spa, garden, elegant rooms, and personalized services.
5. **The Wittmore (Barcelona, Catalonia)**: Located in Gothic Quarter, offering an intimate atmosphere, stylish rooms, a rooftop terrace, and a cocktail bar.

2. Hostels & Budget Accommodations:

- **Hostels:**
  1. **Generator Hostel Barcelona (Barcelona, Catalonia)**: Trendy hostel with dormitory rooms, private rooms, communal spaces, a bar, and social events.
  2. **Sungate One (Madrid)**: Central hostel offering cozy accommodations, a communal kitchen, lounge, and friendly atmosphere.
  3. **Oasis Backpackers Hostel (Seville, Andalusia)**: Located in the city center, offering budget-friendly accommodations, a rooftop terrace, and social activities.
  4. **Equity Point Hostel (Granada, Andalusia)**: Budget-friendly hostel near Alhambra, offering dormitory beds, private rooms, and communal areas.
  5. **Kabul Party Hostel (Barcelona, Catalonia)**: Lively hostel in La Rambla, offering affordable beds, social atmosphere, and vibrant nightlife.
- **Guesthouses & Pensiones:**
  1. **Pensión La Plaza (San Sebastián, Basque Country)**: Family-run guesthouse offering cozy rooms, personalized services, and a central location.
  2. **Hostal La Fontana (Madrid)**: Budget-friendly guesthouse in Gran Vía area, offering comfortable rooms, a friendly atmosphere, and city views.
  3. **Pensión Doña Trinidad (Seville, Andalusia)**: Located in Santa Cruz district, offering affordable rooms,

traditional Andalusian charm, and hospitality.
4. **Hostal Europa (Barcelona, Catalonia)**: Established in 1775, offering budget accommodations, historic charm, and a central location.
5. **Pensión Suecia (Valencia, Valencia)**: Family-run guesthouse offering comfortable rooms, friendly services, and proximity to attractions.

3. Vacation Rentals & Apartments:

- **Apartments & Condos:**
  1. **BarcelonaForRent The Central Place (Barcelona, Catalonia)**: Modern apartments in the city center, offering self-catering amenities, comfort, and convenience.
  2. **Madrid Central Suites (Madrid)**: Located near Puerta del Sol, offering stylish apartments, fully-equipped kitchens, and city views.
  3. **Seville Luxury Rentals (Seville, Andalusia)**: Providing a selection of upscale apartments, penthouses, and lofts in historic districts.
  4. **Valenciaflats Centro Ciudad (Valencia, Valencia)**: Offering contemporary apartments, studios, and penthouses with amenities, comfort, and a central location.
  5. **Mallorca Collection (Palma de Mallorca, Balearic Islands)**: Providing a variety of vacation rentals, villas, and apartments across Mallorca's coastline and countryside.
- **Villas & Country Houses:**
  1. **Villa Padierna Palace Hotel (Marbella, Andalusia)**: Luxury villas, golf courses, spa, and exclusive amenities overlooking the Mediterranean Sea.
  2. **Finca Cortesin Hotel, Golf & Spa (Casares, Andalusia)**: Offering luxury villas, golf courses, spa, and personalized services in a serene setting.

3. **Son Brull Hotel & Spa (Pollensa, Balearic Islands)**: Luxury country house hotel offering villas, spa, gourmet dining, and panoramic views of the countryside.
4. **Villa Retreats (Ibiza, Balearic Islands)**: Providing a selection of luxury villas, estates, and country houses across Ibiza's coastal and countryside regions.
5. **Rural Andalusian Villas (Andalusia)**: Offering a selection of charming country houses, villas, and rural retreats across Andalusia's picturesque landscapes.

4. Paradores & Historic Lodgings:

- **Paradores:**
  1. **Parador de Granada (Granada, Andalusia)**: Located within the Alhambra complex, offering historic accommodations, gardens, and panoramic views.
  2. **Parador de Santiago de Compostela (Santiago de Compostela, Galicia)**: Housed in a former royal hospital, offering historic rooms, cloister views, and pilgrim traditions.
  3. **Parador de Alcalá de Henares (Alcalá de Henares, Madrid)**: Located in a restored 17th-century convent, offering historic charm, gardens, and luxury accommodations.
  4. **Parador de Cuenca (Cuenca, Castilla-La Mancha)**: Offering breathtaking views, historic accommodations, and proximity to Cuenca's Hanging Houses.
  5. **Parador de Ronda (Ronda, Andalusia)**: Located in a renovated 18th-century mansion, offering historic rooms, views of the Tajo Gorge, and luxury amenities.
- **Historic Lodgings & Heritage Hotels:**
  1. **Hotel Palacio de los Navas (Granada, Andalusia)**: Housed in a 16th-century palace, offering historic charm, elegant rooms, and a central location.
  2. **Hotel Casa 1800 Sevilla (Seville, Andalusia)**: Located

in Santa Cruz district, offering historic accommodations, a rooftop terrace, and Andalusian charm.
3. **Hotel Neri Relais & Châteaux (Barcelona, Catalonia)**: Housed in a medieval palace, offering luxury accommodations, gourmet dining, and historic ambiance.
4. **Hotel Hospes Palacio del Bailío (Córdoba, Andalusia)**: Located in a restored palace, offering historic rooms, gardens, spa, and luxury amenities.
5. **Hotel Mercer Sevilla (Seville, Andalusia)**: Located in the historic center, offering luxury accommodations, a rooftop terrace, and Roman mosaics.

5. Campsites & Glamping:

- **Campsites:**
  1. **Camping El Garrofer (Sitges, Catalonia)**: Located near Sitges beach, offering pitches, bungalows, pool, and family-friendly amenities.
  2. **Camping Playa Joyel (Noja, Cantabria)**: Beachfront campsite offering pitches, bungalows, aquatic park, and activities.
  3. **Camping La Marina (Alicante, Valencia)**: Located near Elche, offering pitches, bungalows, aquatic park, and family-friendly services.
  4. **Camping Resort Sanguli Salou (Salou, Catalonia)**: Family-friendly campsite offering pitches, bungalows, pool, and entertainment.
  5. **Camping Armanello (Benidorm, Valencia)**: Located near Benidorm's beaches, offering pitches, bungalows, pool, and amenities.
- **Glamping:**
  1. **Bubbletent Australia (Capertee Valley, New South Wales)**: Offering transparent bubble accommodations for stargazing and nature immersion.

2. **Campera Hotel Burbuja (Valle de Guadalupe, Mexico)**: Providing bubble hotel accommodations amidst vineyards for wine enthusiasts.
3. **Attrap'Rêves (France)**: Offering transparent bubble accommodations in various locations for stargazing and romantic getaways.
4. **Finn Lough Resort (Northern Ireland)**: Providing bubble domes, forest dwellings, and luxury accommodations amidst nature.
5. **Campera Hotel Boutique (Valle de Guadalupe, Mexico)**: Offering bubble rooms, vineyard views, and wine-centric experiences.

Chapter 6:
Cultural Activities in Spain

Spain has a wealth of cultural experiences that allow tourists to fully engage with the history, customs, arts, and legacy of the nation. These are 15 cultural pursuits that tourists might partake in while in Spain:

1. Flamenco Shows:

Discover the passion and ferocity of flamenco, a classic Spanish dancing, singing, and guitar performance. Go to a flamenco show in one of the major tablaos or small theaters in towns like Seville, Granada, Madrid, or Barcelona to see enthralling performances.

2. Visit Historic Palaces and Monuments:

Discover the rich history, architecture, and cultural legacy of Spain by touring its beautiful palaces, castles, and monuments, like the Sagrada Família in Barcelona, the Alhambra in Granada, the Royal Palace in Madrid, and the Alcázar in Seville.

3. Attend Festivals and Fiestas:

Take part in colorful fiestas and festivals held all throughout Spain, including Pamplona's Running of the Bulls, Buñol's La Tomatina, Seville's Feria de Abril, or Valencia's Las Fallas, to enjoy local cuisine, music, dance, and parades.

4. Explore Museums and Art Galleries:

Explore well-known museums and art galleries in Spain, such as the Picasso Museum and Joan Miró Foundation in Barcelona, the Prado Museum and Reina Sofía Museum in Madrid, and other venues that feature modern art, masterpieces, and cultural events.

5. Wine Tasting and Vineyard Tours:

In Spain's well-known wine areas, including La Rioja, Ribera del Duero, Priorat, or Penedès, take part in wine tasting and vineyard excursions where you can explore vineyards and cellars and sample fine Spanish wines paired with regional fare.

6. Culinary Workshops and Cooking Classes:

By taking part in cooking lessons, gourmet workshops, or food tours, you may learn about Spanish cuisine and culinary traditions while exploring regional recipes, ingredients, and preparation methods with local chefs and experts.

7. Explore Historic Neighborhoods:

Explore the small alleys, old buildings, quaint squares, and local shops as you stroll through Spain's ancient neighborhoods and districts, such as the Gothic Quarter in Barcelona, La Latina in Madrid, Santa Cruz in Seville, or El Carmen in Valencia.

8. Attend Traditional Bullfights:

Experience Spain's controversial bullfighting tradition by attending a bullfight in cities like Madrid, Seville, or Pamplona, witnessing the spectacle, rituals, and cultural significance of this historic event.

9. Flamenco Workshops and Classes:

Take advantage of the opportunity to learn about the history, rhythms, movements, and expressions of flamenco through workshops and classes. You may also learn from experienced artists how to sing, dance, or play the guitar.

10. Explore Moorish Architecture:

Visit architectural wonders that showcase Islamic art, design, and cultural influences, such as the Alhambra in Granada, the Alcázar in Seville, the Great Mosque of Córdoba, or the Alcazaba in Málaga, to learn about Spain's Moorish past.

11. Attend Opera and Classical Performances:

Enjoy world-class performances and cultural events in Spain's renowned venues, including the Gran Teatre del Liceu in Valencia, the Teatro Real in Madrid, and the Liceu Opera House in Barcelona. Experience opera, classical music, and performing arts there.

12. Flamenco Festivals and Events:

Take part in flamenco festivals and events held all across Spain, such the Suma Flamenca in Madrid, the Festival de Jerez in Jerez de la Frontera, or the Bienal de Flamenco in Seville, which feature competitions, workshops, and performances.

13. Visit Local Markets and Bazaars:

Travel around Spain and visit local markets and bazaars including

Seville's Mercado de Triana, Valencia's Mercado Central, Madrid's Mercado de San Miguel, and Barcelona's La Boqueria to see traditional crafts, handcrafted goods, and fresh fruit.

14. Explore Gaudí's Masterpieces:

In Barcelona, you may explore Antoni Gaudí's architectural marvels such as the Sagrada Família, Park Güell, Casa Batlló, and Casa Milà. Learn about his distinctive style, symbolic meaning, and impact on Catalan modernism.

15. Flamenco Museum and Cultural Centers:

Learn about the history, artists, instruments, and evolution of flamenco at flamenco museums and cultural centers in Spain, like the Centro Andaluz de Flamenco in Jerez de la Frontera, the Museo del Flamenco in Seville, or the Tablao Flamenco Cordobes in Barcelona.

Chapter 7:
Nightlife And Festivals In Spain

Bars, clubs, rooftop terraces, flamenco performances, music venues, and cultural events abound throughout Spain, making the country famous for its exciting nightlife. The following are fifteen places in Spain famous for their exciting nightlife:

1. Madrid - Chueca:

If you're looking for a diverse and welcoming nightlife in Madrid, go no farther than Chueca, the LGBTQ+ neighborhood known for its abundance of pubs, clubs, live music venues, and cultural events.

2. Barcelona - La Rambla:

One of the most recognizable features of Barcelona at night, La Rambla is home to a plethora of entertainment options for anyone looking to enjoy the city's vibrant nightlife.

3. Ibiza - Ibiza Town:

The dynamic nightlife culture in Ibiza Town attracts international DJs and partygoers, and it is famous for its world-class clubs, beach bars, sunset parties, and electronic music events..

4. Seville - Alameda de Hércules:

With its eclectic mix of bars, restaurants, cafes, live music venues, and cultural events, Alameda de Hércules is the hippest neighborhood in Seville, known for its exciting nightlife.

5. Valencia - Ruzafa:

Located in the heart of Valencia, Ruzafa is a popular nightlife destination thanks to its unique mix of cafes, galleries, live music venues, and pubs.

6. Granada - Calle Elvira:

Calle Elvira is Granada's historic street, renowned for its lively nightlife with traditional tapas bars, flamenco venues, live music, and cultural events, offering visitors an authentic and vibrant atmosphere.

7. Palma de Mallorca - Paseo Marítimo:

The active nightlife scene facing the Mediterranean Sea can be found along Paseo Marítimo, a promenade in Palma de Mallorca that features waterfront bars, clubs, restaurants, live music venues, beach clubs, and more.

8. Bilbao - Casco Viejo:

Casco Viejo is Bilbao's historic district, offering a vibrant nightlife with traditional bars, taverns, live music venues, pintxos bars, and cultural events in a charming and lively atmosphere.

9. Malaga - Muelle Uno:

The waterfront district of Muelle Uno in Malaga is home to hip eateries, cafes, beach clubs, live music venues, and a pulsating nightlife scene, all while boasting breathtaking views of the sea and an exciting ambiance.

10. Alicante - El Barrio:

El Barrio is Alicante's historic district, renowned for its vibrant nightlife with traditional tapas bars, flamenco venues, live music, cultural events, and a lively atmosphere for visitors to enjoy.

11. San Sebastián - Parte Vieja:

Parte Vieja is San Sebastián's old town, offering a vibrant nightlife with pintxos bars, taverns, traditional cider houses, live music venues, and cultural events in a lively and charming atmosphere.

12. Marbella - Puerto Banús:

Affluent pubs, clubs, beach clubs, restaurants, live music venues, and a lively nightlife scene draw celebrities and tourists from all over the globe to Puerto Banús, the luxury marina of Marbella.

13. Tenerife - Playa de las Américas:

Playa de las Américas is Tenerife's renowned nightlife hub, offering a vibrant scene with beach clubs, bars, clubs, live music venues, entertainment complexes, and a lively atmosphere for visitors to enjoy.

14. Zaragoza - El Tubo:

Affluent pubs, clubs, beach clubs, restaurants, live music venues, and a lively nightlife scene draw celebrities and tourists from all over the globe to Puerto Banús, the luxury marina of Marbella.

15. Córdoba - Calleja de las Flores:

Visitors to Córdoba can't miss the busy nightlife along the gorgeous Calleja de las Flores, which features flamenco clubs, traditional taverns, live music, cultural events, and an enchanting ambiance.

Festivals

Colorful parades, energetic music, traditional dances, mouthwatering food, and celebratory atmospheres characterize Spain's colorful and varied festivals, which honor cultural, historical, religious, and seasonal traditions. Tourists to Spain can take part in the following fifteen festivals:

1. Feria de Abril (Seville):

Colorful casetas (tents), flamenco performances, traditional dances, bullfighting, horse displays, live music, and celebratory celebrations with people dressed in traditional garb characterize Feria de Abril, the legendary spring fair of Seville.

2. San Fermín (Pamplona):

San Fermín is Pamplona's famous festival, known for its Running of the Bulls, where participants run alongside bulls through the city's streets, accompanied by parades, music, dancing, fireworks, and cultural events honoring the city's patron saint.

3. La Tomatina (Buñol):

Tourists from all over the globe flock to Buñol for La Tomatina, the world-famous tomato-throwing event, to witness the enormous tomato fight, music, dancing, parades, and joyous celebrations that accompany it.

4. Semana Santa (Various Cities):

During Semana Santa, cities around Spain such as Seville, Málaga, Valladolid, and Granada host religious processions, elaborate floats, hooded penitents, traditional music, somber ceremonies, and cultural events.

5. Carnival (Tenerife & Cádiz):

Cities around Spain, including Tenerife, Cádiz, Santa Cruz, and Las Palmas de Gran Canaria, celebrate Carnival with lively parties, flamboyant parades, costumes, music, dancing, street acts, and cultural events.

6. Fiesta de San Juan (Various Coastal Cities):

Fiesta de San Juan is a midsummer celebration held in coastal cities, featuring bonfires, fireworks, beach parties, traditional rituals, music, dancing, and festive celebrations to welcome the summer season.

7. Feria de Málaga (Málaga):

Flamenco acts, traditional dances, horse shows, live music, fireworks, and colorful tents are just a few of the highlights of Málaga's lively summer fair, Feria de Málaga. The event also pays tribute to the city's rich cultural history.

8. Las Fallas (Valencia):

Las Fallas is Valencia's famous festival, featuring colorful sculptures (fallas), parades, fireworks, music, traditional dances, street parties, and cultural events culminating in the burning of the fallas to welcome spring.

9. Feria de San Isidro (Madrid):

Feria de San Isidro is Madrid's spring festival, featuring bullfighting, traditional dances, music, concerts, street performances, cultural events, and festive celebrations honoring the city's patron saint.

10. Feria de la Virgen del Carmen (Andalusia):

Feria de la Virgen del Carmen is celebrated in coastal towns of Andalusia, featuring maritime processions, boat parades, traditional dances, music, seafood festivals, and cultural events honoring the Virgin of Carmen, the patron saint of fishermen.

11. Semana Grande (Bilbao):

Semana Grande is Bilbao's main festival, featuring concerts, fireworks, traditional sports, Basque dances, music, cultural events, street performances, and festive celebrations attracting visitors from around the world.

12. Aste Nagusia (San Sebastián):

Fireworks, concerts, traditional dances, music, cultural activities, street performances, and Basque sports are all part of San Sebastián's Aste Nagusia festival, which is a joyous celebration of the city's history and culture.

13. Feria de Pedro Romero (Ronda):

The traditional festival of Ronda, known as Feria de Pedro Romero, is a time for remembering the great bullfighter Pedro Romero with festivities that include flamenco performances, traditional dances, music, horse displays, cultural activities, and festivals.

14. Feria de Almería (Almería):

Feria de Almería is a vibrant festival, featuring music, dancing, cultural events, horse shows, traditional activities, and festive celebrations honoring the city's culture, heritage, and traditions.

15. Festival Internacional de Benicàssim (Benicàssim):

Music fans from all over the globe go to the prestigious Festival Internacional de Benicàssim for its world-class performances, camping, cultural activities, and lively celebrations.

Chapter 8:
Souvenirs And Shopping in Spain

Visitors to Spain can enjoy a wide variety of shopping experiences thanks to the country's numerous marketplaces, which provide a delicious mix of traditional handicraft, high-street fashion, gourmet food, distinctive souvenirs, and luxury brands. A brief rundown of the best places to shop in Spain is as follows:

1. Luxury Shopping:

Madrid, Barcelona, Marbella, and Valencia are just a few of Spain's famously posh shopping spots where you can find world-renowned designer labels, posh boutiques, posh department stores, and premium shopping districts.

2. High-Street Fashion:

Shop for the latest trends in women's and men's clothing, shoes, accessories, and makeup at any of Spain's many chic shops, malls, and commercial areas.

3. Traditional Crafts and Artisanal Products:

Discover Spain's rich cultural heritage with traditional crafts, artisanal products, handmade goods, ceramics, textiles, leather goods, jewelry, and unique souvenirs available in local markets, craft fairs, and specialty shops across the country.

4. Gourmet Products and Culinary Delights:

Enjoy the finest of Spanish cuisine in one of the many gourmet markets, food halls, or specialized stores in Madrid, Barcelona, San Sebastián, or Seville, where you can also get local specialties, wines, olive oils, cheeses, cured meats, spices, chocolates, and other unique items.

5. Markets and Flea Markets:

Markets such as El Rastro in Madrid, Mercat de Sant Antoni in Barcelona, and Mercat Central in Valencia provide a lively setting for shoppers to peruse a wide variety of goods, including antiques, collectibles, vintage items, apparel, accessories, souvenirs, arts, and local produce.

6. Shopping Malls and Commercial Centers:

Experience Spain's contemporary shopping centers, commercial avenues, and retail meccas in cities such as Madrid's Gran Vía, Barcelona's Passeig de Gràcia, and Seville's Plaza de Armas. These places offer a diverse array of stores, boutiques, restaurants, entertainment venues, cinemas, and leisure activities.

7. Art Galleries and Antique Shops:

Visit the Golden Triangle of Art in Madrid, Carrer del Consell de Cent in Barcelona, and Ciutat Vella in Valencia, among others, to peruse the extensive collections of paintings, sculptures, antiques, collectibles, and historical artifacts housed in Spain's many art galleries, antique shops, vintage stores, and auction houses.

8. Department Stores and Concept Stores:

El Corte Inglés in Madrid, La Roca Village in Barcelona, and the Ensanche district in Bilbao are just a few of the famous department stores, concept stores, lifestyle boutiques, and multi-brand retailers in Spain that offer a carefully chosen assortment of clothing, accessories, home décor, cosmetics, and one-of-a-kind gifts.

9. Specialty Shops and Boutique Stores:

Discover the one-of-a-kind treasures, sustainably sourced goods, sustainable fashion, and locally crafted wares at Spain's specialty shops, boutiques, independent retailers, and artisan workshops. You'll find these establishments in quaint neighborhoods, historic districts, and hidden gems all over the nation.

Souvenirs

There is an abundance of one-of-a-kind souvenirs available in Spain that reflect the country's culinary, artistic, historical, and cultural heritage. When you visit Spain, make sure you purchase these 15 souvenirs:

1. Flamenco Accessories:

Purchase flamenco accessories such as castanets, fans, shawls, and ornate hair combs, capturing the essence of Spain's iconic dance and music tradition.

2. Spanish Ceramics:

The vivid patterns, detailed designs, and traditional motifs of hand-painted tiles, ceramics, plates, bowls, vases, and ornamental objects from Andalusia, Valencia, and Catalonia showcase Spain's lively ceramic culture.

3. Spanish Wine and Sherry:

The viticultural heritage of Spain is on full display in the world-famous wines, sherries, and cavas produced in areas such as Rioja, Ribera del Duero, Penedès, Jerez, and Priorat.

4. Spanish Olive Oil:

Experience Spain's premium olive oils from regions like Andalusia, Catalonia, and Extremadura, purchasing gourmet bottles or sets to enjoy the authentic taste of Spanish cuisine.

5. Spanish Ham (Jamón Ibérico):

Jamón Serrano and Jamón Ibérico are two of Spain's most famous cured hams; you may buy them in vacuum-sealed packs, gift boxes, or even full legs.

6. Spanish Cheese:

Explore Spain's artisanal cheeses from regions like Asturias, La Mancha, Catalonia, and the Basque Country, purchasing gourmet selections, gift packs, or specialty varieties to savor the country's rich dairy tradition.

7. Spanish Leather Goods:

Find the best selection of Spanish leather items in Madrid, Barcelona, Seville, and Valencia, including shoes, purses, wallets, belts, and accessories made from premium leather.

8. Spanish Jewelry:

Discover Spanish jewelry featuring traditional designs, artisan craftsmanship, precious metals, gemstones, and symbolic motifs, purchasing rings, necklaces, bracelets, earrings, and pendants as wearable mementos.

9. Spanish Ceramics from Talavera de la Reina:

For genuine ceramics, pottery, tiles, and ornamental things showcasing the area's famous blue and white patterns, go to Talavera de la Reina in Castilla-La Mancha.

10. Spanish Gourmet Products:

Delve into the exquisite gourmet products that Spain has to offer, such saffron from La Mancha, paprika from Extremadura, olives from Andalusia, almonds from Mallorca, and chocolates from Asturias. Enhance your culinary experience with gourmet sets, gift baskets, or specialist products.

11. Spanish Textiles and Fabrics:

Fabrics and textiles from Andalusia, Catalonia, and the Basque Country are available for purchase, along with lace goods, handmade blankets, traditional fabrics, and vivid tapestries.

12. Spanish Souvenir Dolls (Flamenco Dolls):

Purchase Spanish souvenir dolls dressed in traditional flamenco attire, capturing the iconic style, elegance, and beauty of Spain's cultural heritage.

13. Spanish Fans (Abanicos):

Explore Spain's exquisite handcrafted fans (abanicos) featuring intricate designs, vibrant colors, decorative motifs, and traditional materials, purchasing unique pieces as decorative items or functional accessories.

14. Spanish Papercraft (Papel Picado):

Discover Spanish papercraft (papel picado) featuring intricately cut paper designs, patterns, and decorative items, purchasing traditional pieces as decorative accents or artistic souvenirs.

15. Spanish Art and Prints:

The towns of Madrid, Barcelona, Seville, and Granada are well-represented in the paintings, prints, posters, and replicas sold at local art galleries, artisan workshops, and souvenir stores.

Chapter 9:
Tips For Traveling in Spain

Spain is a beautiful and fascinating country to visit, and there are many ways to save time and money while traveling there. Here are a few suggestions to help you make the most of your vacation. Travelers to Spain would benefit from the following advice:

Time-Saving Tips:

1. **Plan Your Itinerary:** To make the most of your time and see famous sites, museums, and attractions at their best, it's a good idea to make a flexible itinerary with all of your must-see locations, activities, and experiences.
2. **Use Public Transportation:** Save time and avoid traffic jams by taking advantage of Spain's well-developed public transit infrastructure, which includes trains, metros, buses, and trams.
3. **Book Skip-the-Line Tickets:** To save time and make the most of your sightseeing possibilities, consider purchasing skip-the-line tickets, guided tours, or priority access permits to major attractions, museums, monuments, and landmarks.
4. **Explore Early or Late:** For a more peaceful experience and better photo ops, try visiting popular tourist spots first thing in the morning or last thing at night, when there are fewer people around.
5. **Optimize Accommodation Location:** To save time commuting, explore on foot, and immerse yourself in the local culture and atmosphere, choose hotels that are ideally placed near main attractions, transportation hubs, restaurants, and facilities.
6. **Use Mobile Apps:** You may improve your trip experience and keep organized by downloading travel applications, navigation tools, and digital resources. These will provide

you with maps, directions, transportation schedules, restaurant recommendations, local insights, and real-time updates.
7. **Pack Light and Smart:** If you want to simplify your packing process, make it easier to move around, and save time on transit, versatile clothing, comfy shoes, travel accessories, and little luggage are all great options.

Money-Saving Tips:

1. **Set a Budget:** Prioritize spending, keep tabs on spending, and cut out unnecessary expenses by creating a practical trip budget that details all of your outlays, including lodging, transportation, food, activities, souvenirs, and other miscellaneous charges.
2. **Travel Off-Peak:** In order to save money, get a better deal on lodging, airfare, attractions, and activities—all while enjoying less crowds and a more tranquil atmosphere—plan your trip for shoulder seasons, offseasons, or mid-week.
3. **Explore Free Attractions:** For those looking to keep their vacation budget in check while exploring Spain, there are plenty of free attractions, landmarks, parks, gardens, plazas, beaches, and cultural experiences to choose from.
4. **Dine Local:** Explore local markets, tapas bars, cafes, restaurants, and diners serving traditional Spanish food at moderate prices. Enjoy daily specials, set meals, and value-for-money options without sacrificing taste or quality.
5. **Purchase City Cards:** Consider purchasing city cards, tourist passes, or museum passes offering discounts, savings, and benefits on transportation, attractions, museums, tours, activities, and experiences in major cities like Madrid, Barcelona, Seville, and Valencia.
6. **Stay in Budget Accommodations:** Select inexpensive lodgings such as hostels, guesthouses, bed & breakfasts, vacation rentals, and budget hotels that provide central

locations, low rates, and essential facilities for visitors on a tighter budget.
7. **Shop Smart:** Explore local markets, flea markets, artisans, and independent retailers to purchase souvenirs, gifts, crafts, textiles, ceramics, and gourmet products at reasonable prices, bargaining where appropriate, and supporting local businesses.

Conclusion

Exploring Spain as a German or European visitor is a wonderful way to discover both the familiar and unique aspects of European culture. You'll have an enlightening journey through varied landscapes, ancient towns, lively traditions, and delicious food. Spain is waiting to be explored by all who are drawn to its sunny beaches, architectural wonders, artistic heritage, and picturesque landscapes. Whether it's the artistic heritage of Madrid's museums, the artistic heritage of Barcelona, or the picturesque landscapes of Andalusia and the Balearic Islands, Spain offers a unique blend of experiences.

German tourists can make deep connections with local communities, experience the real rhythms, tastes, and landscapes of this fascinating nation, and create unforgettable memories by embracing Spain's rich history, culture, cuisine, and hospitality. Spain provides a wide variety of places, activities, and experiences to suit any traveler's tastes, interests, and style, whether they're looking to unwind, explore, dine, or party the night away.

Whether you're a German traveler looking to experience the warmth, passion, and beauty of Spanish culture, traditions, and landscapes; appreciate shared European values; celebrate cultural diversity; or just want to learn more about the history, geography, art, and architecture of Spain, there are many aspects of a trip to Spain that a German traveler can enjoy.

Finally, German and European tourists are invited to explore, discover, and embrace the timeless charm, rich legacy, and dynamic spirit of this mesmerizing country as they embark on adventures in Spain. The country offers a unique blend of experiences, chances, and adventures. ©Tengas un viaje inolvidable en España! Aprovecha tu viaje! Go to Spain and have the time of your life!

www.ingramcontent.com/pod-product-compliance
Lightning Source LLC
LaVergne TN
LVHW020139080526
838202LV00048B/3975